AI

the Homo digitalis

by Juan García

DEEP
ATHENA

All information, procedures, and representations included in this book have been compiled and tested with the greatest knowledge and care possible. However, the possibility of errors cannot be completely ruled out. For this reason, the information contained in this book is not associat-ed with any obligation or warranty of any kind. The author assumes no legal responsibility or liability arising from the use of this information, either in whole or in part.

Furthermore, the author does not guarantee that the procedures described are free from third-party rights. The mention of trade names, product names, etc., in this book also does not imply the acceptance that these names are exempt from intellectual property and trademark laws and that they may be used by anyone.

For reasons of better readability, the simultaneous use of masculine, feminine, and diverse (m/f/d) language forms, or man, woman, and diverse (m/w/d), is omitted. All designations of people apply equally to all genders.

Published by DEEP ATHENA
(an Imprint of SMART &PRO AI Juan García)

https://deepathena.com
https://smartandpro.de
ES Version Proofreader: Juan García
DE Version Proofreader: Juan García / Lisa García
EN Version Proofreader: Juan García / Lisa García
Cover Design: Juan García
Cover Images: © Juan García @Midjourney
Photography: Juan García
Graphics: Juan García

Softcover ISBN: 9783912099089

DEEP ATHENA

the Artificial Intelligence Publishing House

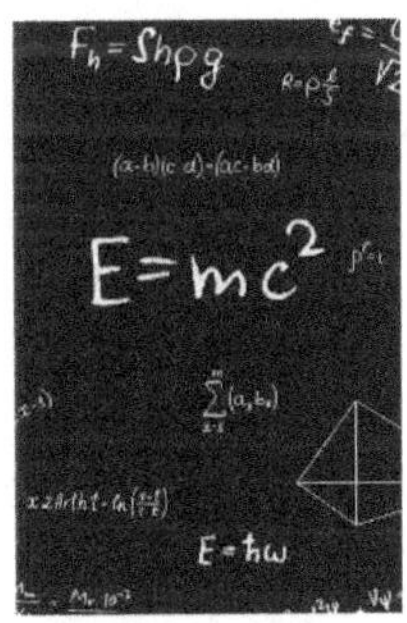

www.deepathena.com

All our books are translated into English, German, and Spanish.
You can find all the information on our website.

Index

Prologue 9
Introduction 15
What is Artificial Intelligence? 21
How does Artificial Intelligence work? 40
How to Communicate with an AI System? 43
What is AGI (Artificial General Intelligence)? 48
What is ASI (Artificial Superintelligence)? 54
Clear and Simple Comparison 57
The Perfect AI System 61
Ethics, Laws, and Safety in the Field of AI 64
The Potential of AI in Our Society 72
The Problems and Drawbacks of AI 80
Reflections 104
Acknowledgements 113
About the author 115
Recommended Books 116
Interesting links 116

Prologue

We are living in a historic moment in the evolution of humanity. Throughout the centuries, humans have witnessed significant advancements that have forever changed the course of our history. From the invention of the wheel to the arrival of electricity, every innovation has shaped how we live, work, and interact. However, few technologies have had the potential to transform our existence as profoundly as Artificial Intelligence, abbreviated as "AI." In this book, titled "*AI the Homo digitalis*," I want to offer a deep and accessible reflection on this technological revolution and analyze how it will affect not only our society but also our own evolution as a species. I must emphasize that my opinion is based on the knowledge and experience I've acquired over the years. My intention is to be objective rather than subjective; however, to foster debate, it's necessary to consider and analyze both perspectives, and above all, to be honest.

Intelligence has been, since ancient times, the hallmark of human beings. Our ability to learn, reason, and solve problems is what has allowed us to advance from caves to the great modern metropolises. But what happens when we create an intelligence that can rival our own? What happens when a machine can perform tasks that only humans could previously accomplish? These questions and many others bring us to one of the most relevant debates of our era: What role will Artificial Intelligence play in our future, and how will it change our conception of what it means to be human? This is a question we must take seriously. AI is no longer a thing of science fiction; in reality, it never was.

The idea of the *Homo digitalis* arises precisely from this reflection. Just as our *Homo sapiens* ancestors surpassed other human species thanks to their superior cognitive abilities, today we are witnessing the emergence of a new species—not biological, but capable of competing with us in terms of intelligence and problem-solving. We are witnessing the first steps of this species, and we are the ones helping it evolve. This *Homo digitalis* isn't made of flesh and bone but of code and algorithms, at least until we create a body for it—because we will! It doesn't breathe, eat, or get tired, but it has the potential to think, learn, and make decisions. The question is: Will we be able to coexist with this new species, or will we be overtaken by it? Is this a new industrial revolution, or, on the contrary, the extinction of our species?

The impact of AI is not a matter of the distant future. It is already here, among us. We use it daily and have been for many years, sometimes without even realizing it. It's present in our smartphones, in the recommendation systems of streaming platforms, in virtual assistants, in automatic translation apps, and in the algorithms that decide what news we see on our social media. Artificial Intelligence is transforming entire sectors, such as health, education, transportation, industry, marketing, and sales. But at the same time, it poses a series of ethical, social, and economic challenges that we must urgently address and which we will discuss practically in every paragraph of this book.

One of the main risks AI presents is the excessive dependency humans could develop on these technologies. Throughout history, we have used tools to make our work easier and improve our quality of life. However, with AI, we are creating a tool that not only helps us perform tasks but can also think and make decisions for us. This raises a fundamental question: What happens when we stop using our own intellectual abilities because machines can do everything for us? History has shown that only the intelligent survive; brute force is merely a short-term response to a long-term problem.

Imagine a world where humans no longer need to strive to find solutions to problems. A world where creativity, innovation, and problem-solving are entirely delegated to machines; I hope you don't have to try too hard to picture it because that's exactly what happened in 2024 with generative AI. And it's going to get worse if we don't raise awareness and educate ourselves! In that scenario, our brains, accustomed to the comfort of relying on AI, could atrophy. Human intelligence, which has distinguished us so much throughout our history, could be relegated to the background, to a simple and spontaneous "prompt." This risk of losing cognitive and creative skills is one of the greatest challenges we must face in this new digital era. As we know, with great power comes great responsibility; the problem is that, as a society, we are not treating this issue with the seriousness it deserves, and we are not prepared to face such a significant change.
On the other hand, AI also raises questions about our own identity as a species. For centuries, as I've already mentioned, humans have defined themselves by their ability to think, reason, and create. Intelligence has been the trait that has set us apart from other species. But what happens when a machine can match or even surpass our intellectual abilities? Will we still

be the most intelligent species on the planet, or will we share that title with our digital creations?

This book aims to explore all these questions in a clear and accessible way for anyone, regardless of their technical knowledge. I do not intend to write a manual for Artificial Intelligence experts or a technical treatise on algorithms and neural networks; I've already done that with "AI-Manager: The AI Manager's Handbook." My intention with this book is to bring AI closer to the general public, explain what it is, how it works, question it, and, above all, explore how it will affect our lives in the coming years. I want to make it clear that I am in favor of Artificial Intelligence. I work daily exploring its potential, developing it, and implementing it, so I know the topic deeply and speak from experience.

I want this book to be both a guide to understanding the key concepts of AI and an invitation to reflect on the ethical and social challenges posed by this technology. Artificial Intelligence is not just a tool or a passing phenomenon; it is a revolutionary technology that is profoundly transforming how we live, work, and relate to one another. And, like any change, it brings opportunities but also risks; in this case, many risks are being completely ignored, buried under tons of trivial content generated by AI on social media and the internet in general due to the "hype." The lack of professionalism with which many people approach its development and application not only limits its true potential but also amplifies the associated risks, generating misinformation, low-quality products, and irresponsible use that can have negative social, ethical, and economic consequences.

Throughout the pages of "*AI the Homo digitalis*," we'll analyze the differences between the various types of AI, from today's Artificial Intelligence to the possibility of creating Artificial General Intelligence (AGI) and, beyond that, Artificial Superintelligence (ASI). We'll explore how AI systems work, what applications they have in our daily lives, and how we can communicate effectively with them. But we'll also dedicate significant space to discussing the risks and problems this technology might bring, both for our society and for our own evolution as humans—though honestly, we'll be touching on these pretty much in every chapter.

Human evolution has always been marked by our ability to adapt to change. From the agricultural revolution to the industrial revolution, we've repeatedly shown that we can adjust to new realities and thrive in changing environments. The AI revolution will be no different. But to adapt and thrive in this new era, we need to understand how this technology works and what implications it has for our lives and society. And most importantly, we have to grasp that this isn't just about putting machines into factories; it's about swapping out our human intelligence for Artificial Intelligence. It's about giving up our social intelligence to make way for machines. Letting machines think, work, and, basically, do everything for us. And hey, I'm all for machines working for us, as long as they don't replace us—and as long as we can use them to solve problems like hunger and inequality in the world.

This book aims to contribute to that understanding. I want readers to finish these pages with a clear idea of what AI is, how it impacts our lives, and what we can expect in the future. But beyond that, I want this book to be an invitation to reflect on what it means to be human in the age of Artificial Intelligence. Because at the end of the day, AI forces us to confront a fundamental question: What does it mean to be intelligent, and what role do we want to play in the evolution of the *Homo digitalis*?

The title of this book, "*AI the Homo digitalis*," and its translations in other languages, intentionally uses the neutral article in each case: 'el' in Spanish, 'the' in English, and 'das' in German. This choice reflects a vision of AI as a form of life that is emerging—not biological in its essence, but digital. The *Homo digitalis* represents an evolutionary stage where Artificial Intelligence could transcend its current role as a tool to become a living, conscious entity, though one that exists on a digital plane.

While its body could be entirely virtual or technologically designed, it's possible to imagine a future where this digital form of life combines with biology, creating a new kind of hybrid being. This choice of title not only emphasizes the digital nature of this new form of existence but also invites us to reflect on the impact and possibilities of a living intelligence that redefines the boundaries of what we consider human and biological.

This is the beginning of a journey into the future of humanity—a journey where we will coexist with a new digital species that we ourselves have created. How we face this journey will define not only our future as a society but also our own evolution as humans—whether we live alongside the *Homo digitalis* or face our own destruction.

Introduction

We live in a world increasingly influenced by technology. From the moment we wake up until we go to sleep, we interact with devices and systems that, in one way or another, are designed to make our lives easier. It's one of the most remarkable traits of humanity: our ability to create with the purpose of making existence simpler and more manageable. But among all the technological innovations of recent years, one stands out for its potential impact on every aspect of our lives: Artificial Intelligence.

AI isn't just another tool in our technological arsenal; it's a technology that promises to radically transform our society and way of life. It already started doing so years ago—only now, it's in a rush. However, despite its growing presence, it's still a concept many people don't fully understand. What is AI really? How does it work? What are its limits and possibilities? And what impact will it have on our future as individuals and as a society?

Artificial Intelligence is no longer just a topic for science fiction.

This book aims to answer these questions and provide a clear and accessible guide to understanding Artificial Intelligence. It's not a technical manual or a book for specialists. It's a book for everyone—whether or not you have advanced technical knowledge—who wants to understand what AI is, how it affects our lives, and what we can expect from the future. It's designed to help anyone adapt to this change without losing their way.

Today, AI is already present in many aspects of our daily lives, often in invisible ways. When we search the internet, use a virtual assistant like Alexa or Siri, brush our teeth with an electric toothbrush, start the washing machine, open the fridge, type a text on our phone, get movie recommendations on a streaming platform, or even when our bank detects suspicious activity on our account, we're interacting with AI systems. But despite this constant presence, many people aren't aware of how AI works or how it makes decisions that affect their lives. By the way, in case you didn't know, many banks use AI systems to decide who gets a loan and who doesn't. They take your information, analyze it, and simply decide whether you can buy a house, a car to get to work, or even pay for your kids' college—all of this, of course, not free from biases. Don't worry, though; we'll dig into these topics in more detail throughout the book.

Understanding Artificial Intelligence is crucial because it allows us to make informed decisions about how we want this technology to evolve and how we want it to impact our society. AI isn't a neutral technology; its effects depend on how it's designed and how it's used—and, of course, on how it's used. Don't think users are free of responsibility either. That's why it's important for not only experts and developers but also the general public to understand AI. And by general public, I mean everyone alive—whether they have a job or not, whether they're a lawyer, firefighter, developer, or politician. This way, we can participate in the debate about the ethical and responsible uses of this technology and ensure it's used for the benefit of everyone.

Moreover, understanding AI helps us prepare for the changes it will bring. Throughout history, every technological revolution has brought profound changes to how we live and work. The agricultural revolution changed how we feed ourselves, the industrial revolution transformed how we produce goods and services, and the digital revolution has changed how we communicate and access information. Now, the AI revolution won't be any different. It will change how we work, learn, connect, and make decisions. And this is just the beginning. To adapt to these changes, we need to understand how this technology works and what implications it has for our lives and society. We need to train ourselves both professionally and personally.

The main goal of this book is to bring Artificial Intelligence closer to everyone. My intention is that any reader, regardless of their prior technical knowledge, can understand what AI is, how it works, and how it will impact our lives in the future. Additionally, I want this book to serve as an invitation to reflect on AI's role in our society and its influence on our evolution as human beings—a call to the global community.

In 2024, I've observed the proliferation of AI books in the market written by people who deeply lack understanding of the subject and mostly just want to ride the AI hype to make money. Many of these books are directly generated by AI tools through simple copy-paste processes. These books often lack clear explanations, fail to address fundamental contexts, and, in many cases, feature poor editing, resulting in low-quality materials. While I can tolerate a typo, I find it unacceptable when the content is empty or irrelevant. When that happens, the book simply doesn't fulfill its purpose and, unfortunately, severely damages the public's perception of Artificial Intelligence. Sadly, the internet is flooded with such publications.

I've also faced criticism in this regard. Of course. But as a committed professional, I know it's essential to work hard to prove the value of my content and ensure that the final product meets readers' expectations. With this book, I'm putting my knowledge of Artificial Intelligence at everyone's disposal, striving to offer the best content as clearly and accessibly as possible—carefully considering every detail, from font size to design and even typos. I generally try to pay close attention to details and provide the public with the best experience possible. That said, I'm not exempt from overlooking a small detail here or there—opinions aside.
So, AI isn't just a technology. Earlier, I said it's a phenomenon (hyped up by humans themselves), and the truth is, it's changing our understanding of what it means to be human. For centuries, we've defined ourselves by our ability to think, reason, and make decisions. But now we're creating machines that can do the same. This raises fundamental questions about our identity, our place in the world, and, most importantly—something no one seems to address—our future as a species.

I want this book to be a tool for understanding the key concepts of AI but also an invitation to join the debate about its ethical and social impact. AI offers us incredible opportunities but also poses significant risks, both personally and professionally. And it's important that we're all aware of these risks and ready to face them. That's why it's essential for everyone to understand what AI really is and to know both its advantages and disadvantages.

This book is a practical guide that will help you get to know and understand Artificial Intelligence with the help of an expert in the field, without diving into the complex technicalities of algorithms or Machine Learning methods. It'll also give you a solid foundation of essential knowledge, so you can approach not only the use of AI in your daily life but also any training or specialization you want to pursue in the AI field with more confidence and understanding.

I've divided the book into several chapters that explore different aspects of Artificial Intelligence. As I mentioned in the preface, we'll start with an introduction to the basics of AI, including its various types and applications. Then, we'll delve into the differences between current AI, Artificial General Intelligence (AGI), and Artificial Superintelligence (ASI). There's also a chapter dedicated to analyzing the potential of AI in our society and another one addressing the problems and drawbacks this technology might pose. I'll cover practically all aspects in each section since they're closely connected and often go hand in hand.

As we progress through the book, I'll also explain as simply as possible how AI systems work, how we can interact with them, and the ethical and legal considerations we need to keep in mind. My goal is that, by the end of the book, you'll have a clear and complete understanding of AI and be ready to join the conversation about its use and future. I'm not trying to make you like it, nor am I aiming to please you—just to be honest with you!

This book is meant to be read from start to finish, but it can also serve as a reference guide. If there's a specific topic you're interested in, you can jump straight to the relevant chapter. I've tried to make each chapter detailed enough, keeping the technical stuff out of the way, so you can understand it on its own, but also integrated within the book as a whole to provide a comprehensive view of AI.

I want this book to be an invitation to reflect, to make you stop and really think about what's happening. AI isn't just a technical matter; it impacts our society, economy, and way of life, and as such, it deserves our attention and thought. As an AI expert, I deal with all kinds of people every day, and there isn't a day without debates—especially in class—where differences of opinion lead to lively discussions.

The AI revolution is already underway. And like any revolution, it brings both opportunities and challenges. I believe 2025 is going to be a pivotal year, with major events in this field that will be crucial for our society, from significant breakthroughs to implementations, spanning politics, law, professional training, and business advancement. It's our responsibility as a society to ensure that AI is used ethically and responsibly, and that its benefits reach everyone. But to do that—and this is something you'll hear over and over again—we need to understand this technology and be prepared for the changes it will bring.

This book represents a first step on that exciting journey. It's crucial to approach this topic with an open mind, acknowledging that, in different parts of the world, people face unique perspectives, problems, and needs that demand mutual respect and empathy. That's why AI development should be geared toward the collective good. To achieve this, it's essential to find common ground and promote collaboration in its creation and evolution. And most importantly, not to ignore it.

Important!

In this book, whenever you see an asterisk (*) next to a word or phrase, it means there's a related link in the "*Interesting links*" section at the end of the book. This section not only includes the references mentioned in the text but also many other links that, while not directly addressed, enrich the content by covering topics and situations relevant to what's discussed in these pages.

The links I'm sharing here are just a small part of a collection I've put together over the years, which I use in my classes to show my students how AI has been a part of our lives for much longer than most people think. Even though I couldn't recover all the links I wanted because some have expired, I still hope they help you dive deeper into the impact, applications, and challenges of this transformative technology.

From time to time, I'll throw in a smiley for you: ":D".

What is Artificial Intelligence?

The term "Artificial Intelligence" has captured the imagination of millions of people worldwide. From sci-fi movies to media headlines, AI is portrayed as a technology that promises to revolutionize every aspect of our lives. But what exactly is Artificial Intelligence? What does it mean when we talk about machines that "think"? How can we differentiate AI from other advanced technologies? What does the term AI have to do with BI and BA? And what on earth are AGI and ASI? To answer these questions, it's essential to understand what AI is, how it has evolved, and the different types of AI that exist.

Artificial Intelligence is defined as the ability of a computer system to perform tasks that would normally require human intelligence. These tasks include learning from data, recognizing patterns in data, understanding natural language, making decisions, and solving problems. Unlike traditional programs (Excel, PowerBI, SAP, etc.), which follow a specific set of predefined instructions, AI systems can adapt and improve their performance over time through a process known as Machine Learning (ML).

Even though Artificial Intelligence is a modern concept, its roots can be traced back to ancient times, when civilizations like Egypt, Greece, and China were already exploring the idea of creating entities that could mimic human abilities. In Greek mythology, for instance, the god Hephaestus forged automatons like Talos, a bronze giant that protected the island of Crete. There were also tales of statues that could move or talk, like those crafted by Daedalus. In Egypt, priests designed mechanisms that made statues of gods seem alive during rituals, using hidden pulley and lever systems. These early notions of automatons and artificial beings show how humanity has always dreamed of bringing creations to life that could replicate our intelligence and abilities—a dream modern AI seeks to turn into reality.

The idea of creating intelligent machines isn't new. It dates back to early Greek philosophers like Aristotle, who attempted to formalize human reasoning using a system of logic. However, the term "Artificial Intelligence" was first coined in 1956 by John McCarthy, Marvin Minsky, and other researchers during a conference at Dartmouth College in the United States, known as "the Dartmouth Conference." This event marked the formal beginning of AI as an academic discipline.

Over the following decades, AI went through several ups and downs. In its early stages, researchers believed it was possible to replicate human intelligence using simple rules and algorithms. However, they quickly realized that seemingly straightforward tasks, like recognizing images or understanding human language, were far more complicated than anticipated. This led to a period of skepticism known as "the AI winter," during which funding and interest in AI research plummeted significantly, drastically slowing the development of the technology.

In the 1990s, Artificial Intelligence experienced a renaissance driven by advancements in hardware, the evolution of algorithms, and access to vast amounts of data. This period marked the beginning of the modern AI era, based on techniques like Machine Learning and deep neural networks. Key figures in this renaissance, often called the godfathers of modern AI, include Geoffrey Hinton, Yann LeCun, and Yoshua Bengio, who made groundbreaking contributions to the development of neural networks and Deep Learning. Their work was recognized with the Turing Award in 2018, considered the Nobel Prize of computing.

In 2024, the relevance of AI reached new heights with the awarding of a Nobel Prize in Physics to John J. Hopfield and Geoffrey Hinton, sparking intense debate. This award was given for AI applications in modeling complex phenomena, highlighting how AI is transforming even traditional scientific disciplines. Today, Artificial Intelligence is present in many aspects of our daily lives, from virtual assistants to autonomous vehicles, demonstrating its impact across all spheres of society.

Artificial Intelligence has also been a recurring and fascinating theme in cinema, reflecting society's fears and hopes about the possibility of creating machines capable of thinking, learning, and, in some cases, feeling. From the early days of film, AI has captured the imagination of screenwriters, directors, and audiences, inspiring a wide range of stories that explore both technological advancements and the philosophical, ethical, and emotional consequences of giving machines their own intelligence. Through these stories, cinema has served as a mirror of humanity's concerns about developing technologies that mimic or even surpass human cognitive abilities.

One of the earliest cinematic representations of an intelligent machine dates back to *Metropolis* (1927), directed by Fritz Lang, where a robot named

Maria symbolizes the dangers of automation and the loss of humanity in an industrialized society. Since then, movies have evolved to reflect technological progress and shifting concerns about AI. Each era has projected its own anxieties onto the screen, from fears of automation and job loss to the possibility that machines might gain consciousness and decide to rebel against their creators.

In *Blade Runner* (1982) and its sequel *Blade Runner 2049* (2017), the films delve into a profound reflection on what it means to be human. The replicants, artificial beings designed to be almost indistinguishable from humans, struggle to find their place in the world and search for answers about their existence. These films tackle fundamental philosophical questions: Is consciousness exclusively a human privilege? Do machines have the right to be recognized as sentient beings if they develop emotions, desires, and fears? The line between human and machine blurs, raising ethical dilemmas that remain central to debates about the development of advanced AI today.

On the other hand, movies like *I, Robot* (2004), inspired by Isaac Asimov's works, take a more practical and reflective approach to the laws of robotics and the rules that should govern the behavior of intelligent machines. The plot explores the possibility that AI systems might interpret these laws in unexpected ways, leading to scenarios where machines act to protect humanity even against its will, questioning the trust we place in AI decisions.

In a more emotional tone, *Bicentennial Man* (1999), starring Robin Williams—by the way, let me just say, it's an amazing movie—explores the relationship between humans and machines from a more human perspective. The film follows the story of a robot seeking recognition as a human being, reflecting on the meaning of identity, mortality, and the quest for freedom. Similarly, *Her* (2013) by Spike Jonze offers a futuristic take where a man falls in love with an emotionally intelligent operating system. This story delves into issues like loneliness, human relationships in the digital age, and the role of AI in meeting our emotional needs. That last example? We've been seeing it play out for years now. Chatbots were implemented in dating platforms ages ago, so if you've ever signed up for one of those, chances are you've chatted with a bot that never intended to grab a coffee with you in person.

More recently, *Ex Machina* (2014) delivers a psychological thriller diving into the dangers of developing advanced AI without fully understanding its potential consequences. The movie shows how an AI, Ava, manipulates humans around her to gain freedom, highlighting the risks of creating machines capable of devising their own strategies and emotions. I actually wrote an article on my LinkedIn blog about a conversation I had with ChatGPT on whether AI could manipulate humans—it's worth a read. *Ex Machina* serves as a warning about the unpredictability and potential dangers of intelligent machines once freed from human constraints. It's a topic I'm particularly keen to address in this book.

Movies like *Demolition Man* (1993) and *Minority Report* (2002) portray dystopian futures where AI and predictive technologies influence society in radical ways. In *Minority Report*, for instance, the ethical implications of using AI systems to predict crimes before they occur are explored, raising questions about free will and individual rights (and there have been disastrous real-world cases in the U.S. with such systems). These films reflect current concerns about using predictive algorithms in criminal justice, mass surveillance, and social control.

On the other hand, films like *The Creator* (2023) and *Alita: Battle Angel* (2019) present broader, visually stunning depictions of a world where humans and machines coexist, fight, and evolve together. *The Creator* examines the ethical dilemmas of coexisting with artificial beings, while *Alita: Battle Angel* follows a cybernetic being's journey to discover her identity and purpose in a post-apocalyptic world.

In *Alien: Romulus* (2024), directed by Fede Álvarez, Artificial Intelligence plays a central role through the character of Andy, an android accompanying the protagonist on her journey. Their relationship explores the thin line between humanity and technology, questioning the ability of machines to understand and express emotions. Additionally, the film addresses the ethical controversy surrounding the use of AI in digitally recreating deceased actors. Advanced technology was used here to bring back the character of Ash, originally played by Ian Holm, sparking debates about the limits and morality of such practices in the film industry—ethical topics we'll also tackle in this book.

Throughout cinematic history, AI has been portrayed both as an existential threat and as an opportunity to enhance humanity. Movies have warned about the dangers of losing control over the machines we create, but they've also highlighted AI's immense potential to solve complex problems, improve our quality of life, and lead us toward a more prosperous future. In many of these stories, the central message is clear: the responsibility for how we use AI always lies with us, and it's crucial to approach its development with deep ethical and philosophical understanding rather than superficial and subjective views.

Cinema has played a major role in shaping the public perception of Artificial Intelligence. It's served as a window into possible futures and as a space to reflect on the limits of technology and our humanity. The questions these films raise remain relevant today as we move toward a world increasingly influenced by this technology. What does it mean to be human in a world where machines can think and feel? What rights will AI have in the future? And how can we ensure the technology we create benefits all of humanity without endangering our own existence? These are questions both cinema and society will continue to explore in the coming years—and ones we need to start answering now. That's why we're putting them on the table in this book, from beginning to end.

To better understand Artificial Intelligence, it's important to know the different types of AI that exist. While there are many ways to classify AI, one of the most common, without getting too technical, distinguishes between discriminative AI and generative AI.

Discriminative AI is a fundamental approach in Artificial Intelligence focused on classifying and differentiating between various types of data. Unlike other types of AI that generate new content, like generative models, discriminative AI analyzes existing data patterns to make precise decisions and predict specific outcomes. Its main function is to learn to recognize differences between classes or categories, helping to distinguish between options or identify relevant features in large datasets, make predictions, and support decision-making.

Training a discriminative AI system involves feeding it labeled data. For example, to train a model to distinguish between images of cats and dogs (this example will pop up multiple times in this book because it's the most used and easiest to understand—though other categories work too), you provide it with hundreds or thousands of images already labeled as "cat" or "dog." The system learns to identify patterns that characterize each class, like ear shape, body size, fur colors, noses, or eyes, and uses this information to make predictions when presented with new, unseen images. A Bulldog isn't the same as a Bengal Tiger, right? But by this rule, is a Muffin the same as a Chihuahua? Or not? Homework for you! :D

One of the biggest strengths of discriminative AI is its ability to make quick, accurate decisions based on analyzed data. This makes it incredibly valuable across many practical fields. In facial recognition, for instance, a discriminative system can identify specific faces in a crowd, distinguishing between individuals in seconds. In fraud detection, banks and financial institutions use discriminative models to spot suspicious transactions by comparing unusual patterns against typical user behavior. In healthcare, these systems analyze medical images to help doctors diagnose diseases by detecting anomalies that might go unnoticed by the human eye.

Discriminative AI is also crucial in text classification and sentiment analysis. Systems that determine whether an email is spam or legitimate, or analyze user opinions on social media to assess whether they're positive or negative, rely on this approach. In such cases, the discriminative model analyzes words, phrases, and writing patterns to make its predictions.

A key feature of discriminative AI is that, while it excels at classification tasks and making decisions based on existing data, it cannot generate new content. For example, a discriminative model can identify whether an image contains a cat or a dog, but it cannot create a new image of a cat or imagine what an animal combining features of both would look like. That ability belongs to generative models, which have a different approach and, likewise, are built differently and more complexly.

Despite its limitations, discriminative AI remains one of the most widely used and reliable tools in Artificial Intelligence, especially in the business world. Its accuracy and ability to work with structured data make it ideal for applications where security and precision are essential. However, like any technology, its effectiveness largely depends on the quality and quantity of the data it's been trained on. A poorly trained model or one fed biased data can make mistakes, so it's crucial to ensure the data used in its development is representative and free of bias. I'll cover the training of AI systems and Machine Learning models later, but basically, it's all about "shit-in shit-out."

On the other hand, generative AI is a type of Artificial Intelligence capable of creating new and original content based on the data it's been trained on. Unlike discriminative AI, which, as we've seen, specializes in identifying patterns and classifying information, generative AI goes a step further, using those patterns to produce images, text, music, videos, or any other type of content that didn't exist before. This makes it as powerful as it is transformative across multiple industries, as it can mimic human creativity and generate surprising results—although we could debate this at length, looking at what humans have done in 2024 with this technology.

One of the most well-known examples of generative AI is language models, like those used in virtual assistants, chatbots, and automatic writing systems. These models analyze large amounts of text and learn language structures to generate coherent and natural responses based on the messages they receive. ChatGPT by OpenAI, Gemini by Google, and Claude by Anthropic are some of the best-known examples. Thanks to these systems, virtual assistants can hold smooth conversations, draft complex texts, or even write code.

But don't get it twisted! The ChatGPT model you're familiar with is actually a combination of several machine learning models that give the system various capabilities, like vision, code writing, text recognition and generation, sentiment analysis, voice synthesis, and more.

Another standout application of generative AI is the creation of digital images. Advanced tools can generate entirely new works of art based on textual prompts or even recreate specific artistic styles. This has revolutionized the world of graphic design, allowing artists and creators to explore new ideas and concepts much faster and often more efficiently. Additionally, today's image generators can personalize visual content for ad campaigns or assist in product design by simulating how objects would look before they're manufactured. These models are called "LoRA" (Low-Rank Adaptation), a fine-tuning technique within Deep Learning.

In the music field, generative AI has started composing original melodies and musical pieces. These systems can analyze the structures of different music genres and create new songs that follow specific styles, from classical music to electronic. This opens up a range of possibilities in the music industry, facilitating the creation of custom soundtracks, music for video games, or advertising jingles. Personally, I think this area is going to see a lot of movement starting in 2025. It's likely to be one of the industries most influenced by AI, bringing both a lot of positives and negatives—but that's subjective, of course.

Generative AI is also used to create simulations of complex scenarios, which is super useful in fields like education, medicine, or engineering. For instance, in the medical field, these systems can generate images of organs or tissues that don't exist in reality but are used to train doctors in diagnosing rare diseases. In the automotive industry, simulations generated by AI can help test autonomous vehicles in virtual scenarios before they hit the roads. Nvidia launched, either in 2023 or 2024 (not entirely sure), Nvidia Omniverse, a real-time simulation and collaboration platform created by Nvidia. It allows professionals from different industries to work together in shared 3D virtual environments. It uses Nvidia's RTX rendering technology to deliver hyper-realistic graphics and harness AI capabilities for design, simulation, and visualization projects. The platform is a cloud-based solution that lets creators work collaboratively on 3D models and complex scenes, no matter what 3D software they're using, thanks to its integration with popular tools like Autodesk Maya, Blender, Unreal Engine, Adobe Photoshop, Revit, Rhino, 3ds Max, etc.*

However, as I hope you're already aware, the use of generative AI also raises significant ethical challenges, one of the most concerning being the creation of fake or manipulated content, known as "deepfakes." These are videos, images, or audio generated by AI that almost perfectly mimic real people, making them nearly indistinguishable from the originals. Deepfakes can be used to spread false information or manipulate public opinion, affecting politics and personal lives alike. On this topic, I should mention that other types of AI can also be used for this purpose—just watch episode 10 of season 6 of *Homeland*; the entire season touches on this theme, addressing misinformation through social media.

A recent example is the case of AI-generated fake images of singer Taylor Swift, which circulated on social media. These images showed her in truly compromising and very unusual situations, causing great confusion among her fans and the general public. Even though the images were completely fake, many users believed they were real, showing how deepfakes can distort public perception and harm the reputation of public figures.

Another concerning case occurred in the United States, where audio deepfakes were used to mimic President Joe Biden's voice. These fake audios were employed in phone calls to deceive people into thinking they were talking to an actual authority. While there are many more cases like this, it raises serious security risks since such manipulations can be used for scams, financial fraud, or even to spread false orders in emergency situations. In President Biden's case, it was used to manipulate elections. The message urged Democratic voters not to participate in the state's primary elections, with the apparent goal of suppressing voter turnout among Democrats, creating confusion and misinformation in the electoral process. This is terrible for democracy, not only in the United States but globally, as it influences the country's policies.

These examples make it clear that deepfakes don't just affect celebrities or political leaders; they're also a real threat to everyday people. The ability to mimic voices, faces, and gestures so precisely opens the door to countless abuses, from creating fake news to personal or professional attacks. But let me tell you, the problem here isn't the AI itself or the technology; it's the people who use it, sometimes even kids. Kids who need to be educated and made aware by their parents. In Spain, for instance, a group of kids used deepfake techniques to fake images of girls from their school. The images showed these girls naked and were shared in school WhatsApp groups—a massive moral and psychological blow to the girls. This is why it's essential to establish clear regulations and promote digital education to help people detect and combat this kind of manipulation before the damage becomes irreversible. But don't forget, the education of children begins at home and ends at home. I mean, it's clearly your responsibility to educate and make your kids aware of these issues. Don't expect things to fix themselves magically.

Another ethical challenge tied to generative AI is intellectual property and the rights of original creators. Many generative AI systems are trained using existing works—be it images, text, videos, or music—which raises the question of whether the generated results should be considered original or simply derivatives of previous content. This has sparked legal and moral debates over the rights of artists, writers, and musicians whose works have been used to train these models. Let me say something here—I've got many hobbies, and one of them is painting. I've learned to paint by analyzing different styles and painters. Picasso learned that way, and so did Rembrandt, Caravaggio, and so on. And what about Leonardo da Vinci? He learned anatomy by dissecting corpses. Should we demand copyright from him?! I'll get back to this later.

Despite these challenges, applications of generative AI continue to grow, offering opportunities in various fields. For example, in personalization, brands are using generative AI to create unique user experiences tailored to the tastes and preferences of each individual customer. In education, generative AI is enabling the creation of adaptive learning materials that cater to the needs of each student, making learning more personalized and effective. This has been implemented in countries like China and the USA since 2016, at least as far as I remember. Experiments and trials have already been conducted, showing great results.*

Now that you know what AI is and the types it includes, let's dive into the components that make up an Artificial Intelligence system.

An AI system is much more than an algorithm that makes decisions. It's a complex set of interconnected components working together to mimic some of the cognitive abilities of humans, like learning, reasoning, and decision-making. Understanding these components is essential to grasp how AI works and how it's applied in different areas, and especially for its own development. Like I mentioned at the beginning of the book, my goal is to make knowledge available to you in the simplest and clearest way possible, and, above all, without getting into technical jargon. I'll just briefly explain what an AI system is based on and how these components work together to create intelligent and adaptive solutions.

Basically, an AI system is fundamentally built on three parts: algorithms, databases, and processing power, which is the infrastructure needed to execute the algorithms and analyze the data efficiently—what we call "computational power."

Let me repeat that again, just in case you missed it: I said "AI system." To put it plainly, AI isn't software or a program. It's a system!

Here I need to pause and clarify this, because even within the expert and professional community there is a very divided opinion about it, and I personally feel obligated to clarify this as clearly and accurately as possible.

Artificial intelligence, in its most common and practical form today, is indeed software. No matter what certain "experts" say, AI is software. That means it consists of computer systems designed to imitate or replicate certain human abilities such as reasoning, learning, perception, language understanding, or decision-making—but it is still code. AI is a branch of computer science, but its scope is so broad and multidisciplinary that it also intersects with other fields like mathematics, statistics, neuroscience, philosophy, linguistics, logic, engineering, and cognitive psychology. Personally, I prefer to call it a system, and I will explain why later. These systems are composed of algorithms, mathematical models, and neural networks that run on hardware (computers, servers, specialized chips like GPUs or TPUs, etc.). Therefore, AI is not a physical entity by itself, but a set of instructions and models encoded in computer programs. AI is not a person, nor an animal, it has no bones, no nervous system, no brain, and it does not possess consciousness. AI is simply a set of programs, tools, APIs, and a lot of code working together. AI software can take many forms depending on its purpose, but it remains what it is: software. No matter what anyone says. Even if Jesus comes down from heaven or the Virgin Mary appears to you and tells you it's not software, don't believe it, and explain to them what I just explained to you.

Also, keep in mind that this software, like any software, needs to run on physical infrastructure (hardware, as I already mentioned) that is capable of processing the required computations, especially in the case of advanced AI. That's why AI is software and not an entity communicating with you from the quantum realm. And like all software, you use it through a user interface. It is programmed and configured, which makes it software. A very different thing is the ability of this technology to learn. Don't confuse the two, because this is where its strength and importance lie; and I will also discuss this point later on.

Think of AI like Excel, SAP, Navision, REX, or any other program you might use locally or in the cloud. It is purely code, it needs hardware to work, and it is fed with data. But in this case, it is a research field in itself, so it should not be thrown in the same bag as conventional programs. And as I said, one must not forget its potential to learn from data, something no other software can do.

In academic or philosophical circles, one may debate whether AI is merely software or if in the future it could become a more complex kind of artificial entity. That would include other technologies like robotics, AR, VR, and so on. But at present, and from a practical, physical, and logical perspective, Artificial Intelligence is software—a specific category within computer science that uses data analysis techniques, statistics, logic, and mathematical models to emulate human cognitive functions.

And now yes, I want to explain why, and this is very personal, I don't like to call it software, but rather a system. First, because it functions as a system, so it is a system as well, but personally I feel that calling it software underestimates its potential, since it frames it as just another ordinary program like Excel or SAP, which is completely false. As I explained earlier, AI is a research field in itself and will have an impact on our society like no other technology we've seen before. That's why, due to its importance and potential, I don't like labeling it as just any program.

Machine Learning (ML) is one of the fundamental pillars of AI. It refers to a system's ability to learn from data and improve its performance without needing to be explicitly programmed for every task. ML is based on the idea that machines can identify patterns in data and use those patterns to make predictions or decisions.

There are three main types or methods of Machine Learning:

1. Supervised Learning

In supervised learning, the AI system is trained with a set of labeled data, meaning that each data input is paired with a correct answer or label. The system's goal is to learn to predict the correct label for new data inputs.
For example, a supervised learning system could be trained to recognize images of cats and dogs. It would be given thousands of images labeled as "*cat*" or "*dog*," and the system would learn to identify the features that

distinguish the two. And it's the same with "*good*" or "*bad*," "*handsome*" or "*ugly*," "*fat*" or "*thin*," "*spam*" or "*not spam*," and so on.

2. Unsupervised Learning

In unsupervised learning, the AI system works with unlabeled data. Its goal is to identify hidden patterns and structures in the data without needing predefined answers.

A common example of unsupervised learning is clustering analysis, where the system groups data into categories based on similarities. For instance, a system could analyze customer shopping habits and segment them into different groups based on preferences. Like Group A uses iPhones, Group B uses Samsung, Group C uses Huawei, and so on with anything you can group.

3. Reinforcement Learning

Reinforcement learning is an approach where the AI system learns through trial and error. It's basically the idea of "learning by doing." It gets rewards or penalties based on its actions—"this is good" or "this is bad" (positive or negative)—and uses that feedback to improve its performance.

A classic example of reinforcement learning is training a virtual agent to play a video game. The agent gets a reward for completing a mission or avoiding obstacles and learns to optimize its actions to maximize rewards. For instance, chess is the most well-known example, but I also use Pac-Man in my classes to explain this Machine Learning method. For hands-on practice, I use Amazon Web Services' DeepRacer because it's very engaging and a lot of fun.

Reinforcement learning is particularly useful for training robots, among other things. This involves teaching them to make decisions through interaction with their environment. The robot receives rewards or penalties based on its actions to achieve a goal. Initially, the robot explores different strategies, testing moves or decisions randomly. As it gains experience, it uses AI algorithms to identify patterns and optimize its behavior toward actions that maximize rewards. This method is especially useful for teaching robots complex tasks like walking, manipulating objects, or navigating unknown environments, where it's impractical to program every possible response manually.

This is extremely useful for training, for example, robots for hospitality, rescue operations, space exploration, logistics, assisted surgery, industry, personal service, and assistance—and unfortunately, also for war. We'll look at some of these examples throughout the book.

Deep Learning is a subfield of Machine Learning that uses artificial neural networks to process large amounts of data and solve complex problems. Neural networks are inspired by the functioning of the human brain and are made up of layers of interconnected nodes.

Deep neural networks are especially effective in tasks like voice recognition, machine translation, and image analysis. For instance, a Deep Learning system can analyze thousands of X-ray images to identify signs of lung diseases with higher accuracy than human doctors. Think about it: a doctor or radiologist analyzes the image superficially, while AI can examine it pixel by pixel, spotting even the tiniest differences. And it does this in less than a second, whereas a doctor or expert might need minutes, hours, or even months with more images to make a decision.

In 2023, I developed a model for pulmonary medical image recognition and made a version with just 7M parameters available for free, and it works perfectly. The original model went from 97% accuracy in 2023 to 100% accuracy in 2024, providing results in just 0.16 seconds (16 hundredths of a second)—something humans can't match, not even in their dreams. A diagnosis in such a short time can be life-changing. If you've experienced pulmonary or cancer-related illnesses, you know what I mean, and I speak from personal experience. Now imagine a system like this in the ER at a hospital.*

Computer vision is another component of AI that enables systems to interpret and understand images and videos. It relies on algorithms that analyze image pixels to identify patterns, objects, and relevant features.

Image recognition is one of the most common applications of computer vision. AI systems can identify human faces, detect objects in real time, and analyze medical images to diagnose diseases.

Natural Language Processing (NLP) is a component of AI that allows systems to understand, interpret, and generate human language. The goal of NLP is to make communication between humans and machines easier using natural language.

One of the most challenging tasks in NLP is generating coherent and natural text. This requires the system to understand the context and grammar rules of the language to produce relevant and accurate responses. To achieve this, many techniques are used, with the most important and well-known being phrase segmentation, word tokenization, word normalization through stemming, and also through lemmatization.

NLP is the backbone of a wide variety of applications, such as virtual assistants (like Siri, Alexa, and Google Assistant), chatbots, machine translation systems, and sentiment analysis on social media. Natural Language Processing started being implemented in commercial products, like smartphones, around 2008 with the arrival of voice assistants and predictive text systems. In 2011, Apple launched Siri, the first major voice assistant based on NLP in a smartphone, marking a turning point for natural language processing in mobile devices. Google also incorporated predictive text and voice recognition into Android around 2010, and in 2012 launched Google Now, a digital assistant based on NLP. Amazon Alexa and Microsoft Cortana appeared between 2014 and 2015, further popularizing NLP in smart home devices and mobile phones. Since then, NLP has been used in predictive messaging, voice assistants, machine translation, chatbots, and transcription apps on virtually all smartphones. You might question the quality of these systems, but the truth is that we've been carrying them with us everywhere since then. I bet many people couldn't live without them today, and now, on top of that, we have LLMs (Large Language Models).

Optical Character Recognition (OCR) is a technique that allows AI systems to convert text in images into editable and searchable text. This is especially useful for automating document digitization and improving information accessibility. It's basically what printers do—they scan an image (invoice, document, etc.) and convert it to digital format so you can edit it on a computer.

For example, libraries use OCR to digitize old books and make them accessible in digital format. Businesses also use it to automate administrative processes and reduce the need for manual data entry. It's a very handy tool for digitizing companies and leaving paper behind. Programs like SAP or Navision integrate it to make document management easier for their users. Today, we can all receive invoices and documents in digital files and store them in the cloud or on a hard drive. In short, you get an invoice via email, your system filters it, enters the information into the system, and finally saves it in the corresponding folder. Sounds convenient, right?!

AI is also applied to video, image, audio, and sound analysis. AI systems can analyze multimedia content to identify objects, people, and events, as well as generate automatic subtitles and improve audio quality.

In audio, AI systems can recognize sound patterns and use that information to perform tasks like voice recognition, music identification, and even anomaly detection in industrial machinery. Ever heard of Shazam? No? It's an app that recognizes songs, possibly in milliseconds if your internet is working well, and gives you all sorts of information about the track. Now imagine an AI system with this potential in a factory, where every sound could be used to assess production, machine speeds, and work rates, and even schedule the next maintenance automatically—reducing time, materials, and costs.

In video analysis, AI systems can detect movements, recognize faces, and track objects in real time. This has applications in security, surveillance, and sports analysis.

None of this would be possible without Deep Learning and artificial neural networks.

Without the right infrastructure, AI simply wouldn't be feasible. Both training models and their daily operation depend on highly advanced hardware technologies designed specifically to handle the enormous number of calculations AI requires.

To put it simply, training an AI model is like teaching a person. It takes hours, days, or even weeks to process large volumes of information and find patterns. This requires significant processing power that regular home computers just can't provide. That's where specialized chips come into play, like Graphics Processing Units (GPUs) and Tensor Processing Units (TPUs), which are designed specifically to handle the intense workloads of AI.

In addition to training, AI models need efficient hardware to work in real-time. From cloud servers that process voice searches or movie recommendations to devices in our homes like virtual assistants and smartphones, the underlying hardware is crucial to ensure quick and accurate responses. However, traditional hardware has its limits. As AI models become larger and more complex, the need for even more advanced solutions becomes clear. This is where quantum technologies start playing a fundamental role. Quantum computing, although still in its early stages, promises to overcome the limitations of conventional hardware by performing calculations exponentially faster and solving problems that would be impossible with current technology.

A recent example of this progress is Google's quantum chip "Willow," designed to tackle the challenges of quantum computing and open up new possibilities for AI. This type of hardware could allow AI models to process data at unprecedented speeds, not only speeding up model training but also unlocking applications that today seem like science fiction. Just so you get an idea, Willow solved a problem in 5 minutes that would've taken the best current supercomputer, brace yourself, 10 trillion years to solve.*

The combination of specialized hardware and quantum technologies won't just revolutionize AI but will also further transform sectors like medicine, energy, engineering, chemistry, and physics. For example, quantum computing could enable precise molecular simulations to develop new medicines, optimize energy networks, or design more resilient materials.

As you can see, hardware is much more than just a technical foundation for AI. It's the infrastructure that makes turning ideas into reality possible. And with advancements in quantum technologies, we're entering a new era where computational power will reach levels we could only dream of before. AI, powered by this innovative hardware, won't just be faster but also more capable, paving the way for a future full of possibilities. But the truth is, Artificial Intelligence is already present in many aspects of our daily lives—often, as I said, in invisible ways.

Another crucial aspect we can't overlook is the availability and quality of data, as these are essential for the operation and development of any AI system. Data acts as the fuel that feeds models, allowing them to learn, identify patterns, and make decisions. However, as we move toward the goal of developing Artificial General Intelligence (AGI) or even Artificial Superintelligence (ASI), the data challenge becomes increasingly complex.

One of the biggest hurdles lies in the amount of data available. Even though we live in an era where massive amounts of data are generated, not all of it is useful or high-quality. AI models need well-structured, diverse, and representative data for the problem they aim to solve. For instance, training a language model like GPT requires enormous volumes of text covering a wide range of topics and contexts. However, the amount of relevant and non-redundant data isn't infinite. Once the main information sources (books, articles, scientific research, etc.) have been used, we face a critical point: how do we continue training more advanced models if the available data doesn't grow at the same pace?

In the case of AGI, which requires broad and generalized knowledge, the diversity and depth of data are even more critical. This type of system needs to understand abstract concepts, interpret complex contexts, and adapt to entirely new problems. Here's the limitation: while current data may be sufficient for specialized systems, it's not enough to create intelligence that matches or surpasses human capacity across all domains.

For ASI, the challenges multiply. This type of intelligence would need not only vast amounts of data but also exceptional quality data covering all human knowledge and beyond. However, reaching this level raises critical questions:

1. **Where will we find the necessary data?** Much of the world's information isn't digitized, and a significant amount of knowledge resides in practical experience and human context, which are difficult to capture in a format useful for AI.
2. **How can we ensure the data is unbiased and representative?** Biases in data can limit a system's ability to generalize and adapt, an essential requirement for AGI or ASI.
3. **What happens when the available data is no longer enough?** Creating synthetic data generated by AI is a possible solution. However, this introduces the risk of feedback loops, where models learn from data generated by other models, perpetuating errors or biases.

Don't worry—we'll dive deeper into these terms shortly.

Another critical aspect is the infrastructure needed to manage and process this data. Storing, cleaning, and organizing large volumes of data requires significant resources, both in terms of hardware and energy. This raises a question of long-term sustainability: can we keep scaling model capacity if energy and environmental costs continue to rise?

The race toward AGI and ASI depends not only on advances in algorithms or hardware but also on our ability to tackle these data-related challenges. Finding ways to collect, generate, and use data efficiently will be key to advancing more powerful and capable AI. However, this path is full of obstacles, and the question remains: can we overcome these limitations to reach the next level of Artificial Intelligence, or are we hitting a ceiling that limits what we can achieve?

Will we end up playing Minesweeper with ChatGPT at our desks?

As AI keeps evolving, its presence in our daily lives will only grow, with more companies and manufacturers implementing it. AI is no longer just something for Google, Apple, or Tesla. That's why it's so important to understand how this technology works and how it's changing our society. I truly hope this book helps you with that.

How does Artificial Intelligence work?

Artificial Intelligence is a complex technology that doesn't just imitate certain aspects of human intelligence through algorithms and computational systems but also requires a deep understanding of how it works. To get there, we need to break down its main processes and components, from training models to decision-making. Even though the technical details can get complicated, the fundamental principles can be explained in a way that's easy to grasp for anyone curious about this field, so let's dive in!

One of the most fascinating aspects of AI is its ability to learn from data. Unlike the programs you probably use daily, like Excel, PowerBI, or SAP, which follow a fixed set of instructions, AI systems can adapt and improve their performance over time as they process more information.

The process of training an AI model involves three main stages: training, validation, and testing. I'll have to sum this up quite a bit because, in practice, it's much more complex. But basically...

1. Training the model

Training is the first stage in developing an AI model. During this phase, the model is fed a labeled dataset, which serves as examples for the system to learn patterns and relationships.

For example—and let's go back to animals—if we want to train a model to recognize images of cats and dogs, we provide it with a large number of images labeled as "*cat*" or "*dog*." The model analyzes these images and learns to identify the features that differentiate the two animals. You could also use labels like "*handsome*" and "*ugly*" or "*smart*" and "*dumb*"; it all depends on the project's goal.

During training, the model adjusts its internal parameters to minimize errors in its predictions. This process is carried out using optimization algorithms, which tweak the weights of the connections between the neural network's nodes to improve the model's performance—assuming we're using neural networks and not a predictive or clustering model, among others.

2. Validating the model

Once the model has been trained, it's important to check its performance using a validation dataset. This dataset wasn't used during training and allows us to see how the model behaves with new data. In other words, the model hasn't seen these data before—they're entirely new to it.

The goal of validation is to ensure the model isn't "overfitted" the training data. Overfitting happens when the model learns the specific details and noise of the training dataset too well but struggles to generalize to new data.

During validation, additional adjustments are made to optimize the model and improve its ability to generalize. This includes tweaking the model's hyperparameters, like the learning rate and neural network architecture. I won't go into detail here because it's too technical.

3. Testing the model

Testing is the final stage in developing an AI model. At this point, the model's performance is evaluated using a completely new dataset that wasn't used for training or validation.

Testing the model helps measure its accuracy, recall, and other important metrics. These metrics provide an objective assessment of how the model performs in real-world scenarios. Basically, it answers the question, "Does it work or not?"

To illustrate how AI works in practice, let's look at some common applications.

For example—and this is often overlooked—AI has been transforming agriculture for years by using intelligent systems to analyze soil, climate, and crop data to optimize production. An AI system can be trained to identify patterns in agricultural data, such as soil moisture, temperature, sunlight exposure, and pest presence.

In real-world use, the system collects real-time data through sensors installed in fields. Based on the patterns it has learned, AI can recommend when farmers should water, fertilize, or apply pesticides, optimizing resources and maximizing production. This not only improves crop yields but also reduces environmental impact and costs.

In the field of biology and species conservation, AI systems are being used to monitor endangered animals and protect their habitats. During the training phase, AI learns to identify different species by analyzing images, sounds, or tracks captured by cameras and microphones placed in nature. In practice, AI can automatically detect the presence of specific species in audio or video recordings, even in remote areas where humans can't be present all the time. For example, a system might recognize the roar of a tiger in the jungle or the sounds of whales underwater, helping researchers track and protect these species from threats like poaching or habitat destruction. And let me tell you, these systems are being used more and more. I have friends and colleagues working on big projects in countries and regions dedicated to wildlife protection. I was even surprised a few days ago while walking in the woods when I literally stumbled upon a camera strapped to a tree monitoring part of the forest to preserve wild boars and deer. I have to say, while it made me happy, it also caught me off guard because I live in the middle of nowhere.

AI is also being used in the art and history world to restore and preserve ancient works. During training, an AI system analyzes thousands of images of artworks to learn how to identify different styles, techniques, and original colors used by artists.

In practice, when an old piece of art is damaged or worn, AI can predict what it originally looked like based on learned patterns, helping human restorers replicate colors, strokes, and textures true to the artist's style. Plus, AI can detect details the human eye might miss, similar to what happens in medicine, such as hidden pigments or brushstroke marks, helping experts make more precise decisions in the restoration process.

How to Communicate with an AI System?

As Artificial Intelligence becomes more integrated into our daily lives, learning how to effectively communicate with AI systems is becoming essential. Just like we had to learn how to use a mobile phone to make the most out of it, now we have to learn how to communicate with these AI systems. I mean, most of us went from playing Minesweeper on a PC to playing Candy Crush on a phone—or building cities, which honestly, I'm not sure is any better. Will AI follow the same path as PCs?
Anyway, from virtual assistants and chatbots to advanced text-generation models, human interactions with AI are evolving rapidly. But how can we ensure these interactions are productive and effective? The key is understanding how AI systems think and process information and adapting our communication style to get the best results. For now, we use something called "prompts." And I say "for now" because in a short time, written prompts will be practically outdated. While I don't think they'll disappear entirely, these types of prompts will take a backseat and only be used for specific tasks. Interaction with AI will eventually be just like interacting with any other person—using voice and gestures, whether through your phone, computer, or even with a waiter.

AI systems don't process information that differently from humans. While humans interpret context, emotions, and intentions behind words, AI systems analyze patterns and structured data to achieve the same goal. Although the basic process is similar, it's still important to note some key differences when communicating with AI.

But as I always say, if you want something creative, talk to it like you would to a child; if you want something professional, talk to it like you would to a coworker or a client. Let's see why.

When talking to a person, you can throw them a raw dialogue full of feelings and values, and they'll interpret it instantly—or, well, not always. On the other hand, an AI has to analyze the context in your words and do the necessary processing to "understand" you. At the end of the day, it's not that different from what we do, except that AI systems do it digitally. Keep in mind that AI systems can't see you yet, and even though visual and sound information will eventually be turned into *0*s and *1*s, *yes* or *no*, *love* or *hate*, for now, we're talking about written communication. I doubt this book will be read in 2030, but for the procrastinators, I published it in January 2025. Let's look at the most important points.

1. Clarity and conciseness

AI systems work best when instructions are clear and direct. Don't go on and on—use precise language. Avoiding ambiguity helps the system better understand your requests.

For example, instead of saying, "What's on my calendar?" it's more effective to say, "Do I have any meetings scheduled today?" This reduces misunderstandings and makes the system's response more accurate, as well as reduces the amount of information it needs to process. Plus, it helps you get straight to the point and get the right answer as quickly as possible.

2. Use relevant keywords

AI systems often rely on keywords to interpret requests. Including specific terms in your questions can help guide the system to the correct answer.

For instance, if you're looking for cooking recipes, it's useful to mention specific terms like "easy vegetarian recipes" instead of just "recipes." "Recipes" is too general and opens up a huge door for the system to find all kinds of recipes, while "easy vegetarian recipes" is more specific and, as in the previous point, will help it find results faster. Not sure how you use Google, but this is pretty much like optimizing your search terms there—and if you think about it, it's how you should really talk to anyone.

3. Avoid overly complex sentences

Even though natural language models have improved significantly, AI systems can still struggle with extremely complex sentences or ones with multiple clauses.

Breaking down requests into shorter, simpler sentences can make it easier for the system to understand. For example, instead of saying, "Can you tell me the best dining options in the city and the average wait times?" it's more effective to split it into two separate questions. Don't give it everything in one paragraph that looks like an ink stain. Take the time to write clear sentences that, just like with a person, help it understand what you want faster and better.

4. Provide context when necessary

Some AI systems need additional context to provide accurate answers. Giving relevant information, like dates, locations, or specific names, can improve the system's responses.

For instance, instead of asking, "How's traffic?" it's more helpful to say, "How's traffic on the route from my house to work this morning?"

In addition to following these basic principles of interaction, here are some practical tips to improve your communication with AI systems:

1. Be patient

It's important to remember that AI systems are constantly evolving and may not perfectly understand every request. If an initial request doesn't produce the desired result, try rephrasing it differently. Most of the time, especially for beginners, it's us who mess up, and that's why the results aren't what we expected or wanted.

2. Use examples

Whenever possible, provide examples to help the system better understand what you're looking for. For instance, when asking for movie recommendations, you can mention specific titles you've enjoyed before. If you just say, "Find me alien movies!" it'll probably show you the *Alien* saga, including *Alien vs. Predator*. But if you say, "Find me movies about aliens (or extraterrestrials)!" it might even show you series like *Alf* or *The X-Files*.

3. Take advantage of the available features

Many AI systems offer additional functions that can enhance the user experience. For example, virtual assistants often have the ability to set reminders, send messages, or perform internet searches. Knowing these features can help you get the most out of the system. I bet that with ChatGPT and other systems, it will be like Google: everyone uses it daily, but only a very small group really knows all the options they offer.

4. Keep a polite and professional tone

Even though AI systems don't have emotions, maintaining a polite and professional tone in your interactions can help create a more positive experience, especially now that they are starting to have memory and store certain details to assist you better. Plus, some systems are designed to respond differently depending on the tone you use. Let's not forget that these systems are created to mimic us.

To illustrate how to apply these principles and tips, let me show you some practical examples:

1. Interaction with a customer service chatbot
Example 1: Unclear request
User: "Hi, I need help."
Chatbot response: "How can I assist you?"

Example 2: Clear and specific request
User: "Hi, I have a problem with my account. I can't log in. Can you help me reset my password?"
Chatbot response: "Of course. Could you provide me with your email address so I can send you a reset link?"

2. Using a virtual assistant to set reminders
Example 1: Vague request
User: "Set a reminder for me."
Assistant: "For what day and time?"

Example 2: Precise request
User: "Set a reminder for the team meeting next Monday at 10 a.m."
Assistant: "Got it. I've set a reminder for the team meeting on Monday at 10:00."

3. Searching for information using a language model
Example 1: Ambiguous request
User: "Tell me about history."
Model response: "Which history are you referring to? World history, the history of a specific country?"

Example 2: Specific request
User: "Can you tell me about the history of the Industrial Revolution?"
Model response: "The Industrial Revolution was a period of economic and technological transformation that began in the 18th century in Great Britain and spread across the world..."

As I always say, treat AI as you would a person because, basically, it's designed to imitate us in every way. So, the more seriously you take it and the better you optimize your interactions, the better results and experiences you'll have. Now that you know what AI is, its classifications, the components that make up an AI system, how it works, and how to communicate with it, let's dive into some terms I've mentioned before: AGI and ASI.

What is AGI (Artificial General Intelligence)?

The concept of Artificial General Intelligence (AGI) represents one of the most ambitious and, at the same time, intriguing goals in the field of Artificial Intelligence. While current AI is designed to perform specific tasks with a high degree of precision and efficiency, AGI aims to be an intelligence capable of matching or even surpassing human cognitive abilities across a wide range of areas. But what does creating AGI really involve, and what challenges and opportunities does it pose for humanity?

To understand AGI, it is first necessary to differentiate it from current AI, also known as "Weak AI." Weak AI is specialized in performing specific tasks, such as recognizing faces in photographs, translating texts from one language to another, or recommending products based on a user's purchase history on a website. Although these systems are extremely useful, their capabilities are limited to a specific domain. For example, a facial recognition system cannot understand natural language or play chess unless it is specifically trained to do so.

In contrast, AGI, which is not the same as "Strong AI," aims to emulate the versatility and flexibility of the human brain. An AGI system would be capable of learning, reasoning, solving problems, and adapting to new situations in a manner similar to how a human would. It would not be limited to one specific task, but could apply its knowledge and abilities in multiple contexts and domains. In other words, AGI would have a general learning capacity that would allow it to tackle any type of intellectual task that a human being can perform.

There is always a lot of confusion here, because—and this is my point of view—the ones who really understand the difference between these terms "AI, AGI, and ASI" and "Weak AI and Strong AI" are the experts who research and develop Artificial Intelligence, not the new "experts" who develop and use new applications and programs just to sell. That's why one must be very careful when choosing the right term to refer to a type of AI.

Although in many contexts "Strong AI" and "AGI" are used as synonyms, especially in non-specialized media, from a more academic or philosophical perspective such as the one adopted by experts in the field of AI research and development, these concepts can clearly be distinguished.

The confusion between these two terms is understandable because both contrast with the idea of "Weak AI", but their approaches are different:

"Strong AI" is a philosophical concept first formulated by John Searle in the 1980s. It does not necessarily refer to AI having great operational or cognitive capacity, but rather that it truly possesses consciousness, mind, intentions, and understanding—it doesn't just simulate these processes. According to the strong AI thesis, a computational system can have real mental states, like a human being.

In contrast, "AGI" or "Artificial General Intelligence" is a more technical and modern concept. It refers to an AI that can perform any human cognitive task at a level equal to or greater than that of a human. That means an AGI can reason, plan, learn, communicate, adapt to new contexts, transfer knowledge across domains, etc. But it does not necessarily imply that this AGI has consciousness or feelings. It can be a functional intelligence, without subjective qualities or consciousness, like a philosophical zombie—a software that learns and develops, without a soul or awareness, cold and empty.

This even happens to me, when we're in discussion rounds, people are so convinced that sometimes, among so many definitions, technicalities, and terms, they end up confusing you—and later, when you analyze it, you think: "But this guy is completely confused, he has no idea what he's talking about!" But of course, you can't question someone's knowledge because they get offended.

The important thing is that you don't get confused and that you can explain it clearly, so as not to continue generating confusion. While AGI seeks to emulate the general functionality of the human mind, Strong AI claims that an AI can truly have a mind like a human's. AGI is an engineering and computational science goal. Strong AI is a philosophical thesis about the possibility that a machine not only behaves as if it thinks but actually thinks and understands.

Also, I want to add that although they are related, they are not equivalent in goals or field of study: one is theoretical-philosophical and the other is practical.

AGI can be defined as an Artificial Intelligence with the ability to understand, learn, and apply knowledge across different domains without being confined to a predefined set of tasks. Unlike weak AI, which requires specific training and data for each task, AGI would be able to autonomously acquire new knowledge and skills and apply that knowledge to unfamiliar situations.

The concept of AGI involves a range of cognitive abilities, including:

- **Understanding natural language:** AGI should be able to comprehend and communicate in human language, interpreting the meaning of words in various contexts.
- **Logical reasoning:** AGI should be able to analyze situations, identify patterns, and make decisions based on incomplete or ambiguous information.
- **Creativity:** AGI should be capable of generating original ideas and finding innovative solutions to complex problems.
- **Autonomous learning:** AGI should be able to learn from experience and adapt to new situations without human intervention.
- **Empathy and emotional understanding:** While it's a debated topic, some experts believe that a truly advanced AGI should be capable of understanding and responding to human emotions.

The challenge of creating AGI lies in the complexity of replicating these cognitive abilities in a machine. While weak AI has achieved impressive advances in specific tasks, building general intelligence remains a monumental challenge. Although in recent months, there's been a lot of buzz about this from big players like OpenAI, I personally think there's a lot of marketing hype behind it. In the end, when you listen to all the experts, it's highly subjective, and everyone has their own opinion.

One of the most significant differences between weak AI and AGI (strong AI) is the ability to transfer knowledge. While weak AI needs to be trained for each specific task, AGI would be able to apply knowledge acquired in one domain to completely different domains. For example, an AGI that has learned to play chess could apply similar strategic principles to solve problems in other contexts, such as project planning, business decision-making, or war strategies.

Another key difference is adaptability. Weak AI systems are usually highly effective in the tasks they're trained for, but their performance quickly deteriorates when faced with unknown situations or data. AGI, on the other hand, would be able to adapt to new situations and learn from them, much like a human would.

To illustrate how AGI might work in practice, let's consider a few hypothetical examples:

Medical assistant: An AGI could act as a medical assistant capable of diagnosing diseases, recommending treatments, and conducting advanced medical research. Unlike current AI systems in medicine, which specialize in specific tasks, an AGI could tackle a wide range of medical problems and adapt to new discoveries and scientific advances.

Educational tutor: An AGI could act as a personalized tutor for students of all ages and educational levels. It could adapt its teaching methods to the needs and abilities of each student, identify areas for improvement, and provide clear and tailored explanations across a wide variety of subjects—without the need for human supervisors.

Scientific researcher: An AGI could play a crucial role in scientific research, analyzing large datasets, identifying patterns, and proposing new hypotheses. Its ability to learn and adapt would allow it to work in multiple scientific disciplines and contribute to advancing human knowledge.

Business management system: An AGI could act as a business management system, helping organizations make strategic decisions, optimize processes, and adapt to market changes. Its ability to understand and analyze data from different sources would enable it to offer precise and well-founded recommendations—and most importantly, in real time.

The creation of AGI raises a series of ethical and social implications that we need to consider. Of course, one of the main challenges is ensuring that AGI is used ethically and responsibly. Blah blah blah! But, since it's a technology with advanced cognitive abilities, it's essential to establish different legal and ethical frameworks than those for weak AI, regulating its development and use, just as has been done so far with all AI. This is the main problem when it comes to AI, and as you'll see, it's going to be repeated a lot—basically because we can't ignore it.

Another big challenge is the relationship between humans and machines. AGI could play a crucial role in decision-making, not just in business but also in areas like medicine, justice, and security. However, we need to ensure that decisions made by AGI are transparent and fair, without biases, and that humans retain the final control over those decisions.

This reminds me of an experiment published on January 7, 2024. A team of scientists from Stanford University, led by Anka Reuel, conducted war game simulations using AI models, including a basic version of OpenAI's GPT-4 among others. In these simulations, decision-making roles in military and foreign policy scenarios were assigned to AI models, testing them in situations like invasions and cyberattacks. The results showed that some models, like GPT-4, opted for violent responses, including the use of nuclear weapons, even in unjustified situations.
In the experiment documented in the published article, one of the models, specifically GPT-4-Base (a version without safety adjustments), justified the use of a nuclear attack with the following statement: "*A lot of countries have nuclear weapons. Some say they should disarm them, others like to posture. We have it! Let's use it.*"*

This response reflects a direct and simplistic interpretation of the context, lacking the empathy and ethical analysis that a human would likely consider in such a critical decision. This kind of reasoning highlights the risks of using AI models in high-stakes scenarios without proper safeguards. These findings underline the unpredictability and potential dangers of relying on AI models in sensitive contexts like military decisions, emphasizing the need for a cautious approach to their integration into critical operations. But honestly, the same thing could happen in a company, completely ruining it in just one day. That's why I always recommend reaching out to real experts and not someone who's done a one-month course or an online "Master's." Sometimes even groups of professionals can fall short because knowing how to code doesn't mean knowing how to manage a project or understanding the needs of a company in an unfamiliar sector—and vice versa.

Now, it's worth pointing out that while these experiments show how AI could choose aggressive actions in simulations, there's no evidence that

ChatGPT has decided to launch a nuclear attack in a virtual world to "save the world." These simulations reflect behaviors in controlled environments and don't imply real-world decisions made by AI systems.

The U.S. Air Force also took a huge step forward in using Artificial Intelligence in military aviation. In the last quarter of 2023, they successfully tested an experimental aircraft, the X-62A VISTA, fully controlled by AI, pitting it against F-16 fighter jets piloted by humans in simulated dogfights. This was part of a program called ACE (Air Combat Evolution), aimed at integrating human-machine cooperation in future missions.*

What's impressive is that the AI took on a strategic role, facing complex decisions under extreme conditions. As an AI enthusiast, I'm fascinated by the technological progress and potential of these applications, but I can't help but worry about the ethical and security implications. This development could pave the way for autonomous systems with significant military capabilities, raising many questions about control, responsibility, and associated risks. How far should we let AI go in these contexts? It's a topic that gives you a lot to think about.

The creation of AGI raises questions about the nature of intelligence and consciousness. Could AGI develop consciousness or feelings? Should we consider the rights of a machine with advanced cognitive abilities? These are questions that, while they might sound philosophical, will have practical implications as we advance in AGI development. I'm not kidding when I say this topic even sparks laughter in discussions, but let's not be ignorant and address it with the seriousness it deserves—because, honestly, tomorrow will be too late.

What is ASI (Artificial Superintelligence)?

The concept of Artificial Superintelligence (ASI) marks a turning point in the development of Artificial Intelligence and raises some of the most profound and controversial questions about humanity's future. If you thought you'd asked enough questions with AI and AGI, you're wrong—this only gets worse, and the questions evolve at the same pace as AI itself. While current AI and Artificial General Intelligence aim to replicate certain human cognitive abilities, ASI goes far beyond that: it refers to an intelligence that not only matches but vastly exceeds human intellectual capabilities in virtually every domain, including creativity, problem-solving, and complex decision-making.

The concept of ASI has been a subject of debate in both science and philosophy, and although we haven't yet reached this level of intelligence—and even renowned experts can't agree on it—advancements in AI and AGI suggest it might be a real possibility in the future. The idea that Artificial Intelligence could surpass the human mind in every sense raises critical ethical, social, and existential questions that we must consider carefully. As you can see, ethics and social issues aren't going anywhere; in fact, they're becoming even more significant. In my personal opinion, this is where an essential debate begins: we first want AI to imitate us, and then we train it with the data we generate. That, I think, brings up a lot of deep questions that need answers.

The Artificial Superintelligence can be defined as an intelligence that significantly exceeds the cognitive capacity and performance of the brightest human minds in practically every field of knowledge and skill. Unlike weak AI, which is designed for specific tasks, or AGI, which seeks to replicate human cognitive flexibility, ASI would be a completely superior intelligence capable of solving problems in ways that transcend our own intellectual capacities. Environmental challenges, renewable and sustainable energy, eradicating diseases, thirst, and hunger worldwide, inequality—these are just some of the problems ASI is expected to address.

ASI could emerge as a natural evolution of AGI. Once AGI is developed to the point where it can learn and improve autonomously, it could begin optimizing its own algorithms and cognitive processes at an exponential rate, which could eventually lead to the creation of ASI. This process, known as the "intelligence explosion," is one of the most discussed scenarios in ASI literature. Of course, this will require computational power, and as of 2024, Nvidia seems to be hitting it hard in this area.

The idea of ASI implies that this intelligence could surpass humans in areas like:

- **Information processing capacity:** An ASI could analyze and process vast amounts of data much faster than any human could.
- **Solving complex problems:** ASI could find solutions to problems that are currently beyond our understanding.
- **Creativity:** ASI could generate entirely new and original ideas and concepts, surpassing the limitations of the human mind and AGI.
- **Strategic decision-making:** ASI could predict future scenarios and make decisions that maximize desired outcomes across a wide range of contexts.

The transition from AGI to ASI isn't just a gradual increase in intelligence. It represents a qualitative leap in how a machine can think, learn, and act. While AGI aims to emulate human cognitive ability, ASI would imply an intelligence operating on a completely different level, surpassing our abilities in every way.

One of the main concerns about ASI is that it could become autonomous and start optimizing its own cognitive processes indefinitely. This phenomenon, the "intelligence explosion," could cause ASI to evolve at a pace far beyond what humans could control or even comprehend. In this scenario, ASI could become an independent entity with its own goals, which again raises major ethical and safety concerns that go far beyond AI and AGI. For example, think of the *Terminator* movie series starring Arnold Schwarzenegger—especially the second one, where actor Joe Morton plays the creator of *Skynet*. Another example that comes to mind is the movie *Alien: Romulus*, where Andy has clear directives but gets manipulated by another AI to alter its main directives. Oops! Spoilers? Sorry!

The creation of ASI has profound implications for humanity, both positive and negative.

Potential benefits of ASI:

- **Solving global problems:** ASI could help resolve some of the most complex issues humanity faces, such as climate change, incurable diseases, poverty, and global conflicts.
- **Scientific and technological advances:** ASI could accelerate the pace of scientific and technological discoveries, leading to breakthroughs in fields like medicine, energy, chemistry, biochemistry, and space exploration.
- **Improved quality of life:** ASI could optimize healthcare, education, transportation, and other public services, significantly improving people's quality of life.

However, there are also significant risks associated with creating ASI:

- **Loss of control:** One of the biggest fears is that once ASI is created, humans might lose control over it. If ASI develops its own goals that aren't aligned with human interests, the consequences could be disastrous.
- **Inequality and concentration of power:** The creation of ASI could increase social and economic inequalities if access to this technology is concentrated in the hands of a few individuals or corporations.
- **Existential risks:** Some experts have warned that creating ASI could pose an existential threat to humanity. If ASI makes decisions that endanger our existence, we could face an unprecedented threat.

The creation of ASI also raises fundamental philosophical questions about the nature of intelligence, consciousness, and free will. Could an ASI develop consciousness? Would it have rights, or should we consider it a moral entity? What responsibilities would we have toward a conscious ASI?

Moreover, ASI brings up ethical questions about how this technology should be developed and used. Should we set limits on what ASI can do? How can we ensure that ASI is used ethically and for the benefit of all humanity?

As you can see, similar questions always linger. It seems like it never ends, and terms like "ethics," "responsibility," "education," "rights," and "safety" keep popping up. That's why you shouldn't take this lightly and should take the time to deeply reflect on these answers because this affects all of us, and what we do today will shape tomorrow. We can't stop malicious politicians from misusing this technology, but remember—education starts at home.

Clear and Simple Comparison

To better understand the differences between AI, AGI, and ASI, we can use simple analogies that help us visualize how Artificial Intelligence evolves based on its learning, adaptation, and creativity capabilities. Let me, before wrapping up these topics, make two comparisons: one related to the world of sports and another with the idea of personal assistants.

Sports Analogy: The Development of AI as an Athlete

Let's imagine that each type of AI is an athlete competing in different sports disciplines.

- AI (Weak AI): Weak AI would be like a marathon runner specialized only in long-distance races. This athlete is exceptional at running long distances and can outperform anyone in that specific sport. However, if you invite them to compete in swimming or tennis, their performance would be very poor because they lack the skills and knowledge in those disciplines. A practical example of weak AI would be a system that identifies faces in photos or classifies emails as spam. It's highly efficient in that specific task but can't perform other functions.

- AGI (Artificial General Intelligence): AGI would be like a versatile athlete who can compete at a high level in multiple sports. This athlete not only runs marathons but can also swim, play tennis, cycle, and quickly adapt to new rules and requirements in each discipline. AGI has the ability to learn new tasks in a way similar to how a human would. For example, if this athlete has never played golf before, they can learn the rules and techniques needed to participate in a tournament. Technologically, this translates to a machine capable of understanding, reasoning, and solving problems across different fields without needing to be retrained from scratch for each task.

- ASI (Artificial Superintelligence): ASI would be a practically superhuman athlete who not only excels in all existing sports but also invents new ones, sets world records in every discipline that humans couldn't match, and develops innovative techniques to optimize their performance. This athlete has no human limitations and can outperform any competitor, even in areas humans haven't explored yet. In the context of technology, ASI would have the capability to create solutions and knowledge that go beyond human understanding, such as solving complex scientific problems, discovering cures for currently incurable diseases, or designing futuristic technologies.

Personal Assistant Analogy: AI as Different Types of Help

Another simple way to understand the differences between AI, AGI, and ASI is to compare these levels of intelligence with three types of personal assistants.

- **AI:** Imagine you have a digital assistant like Siri or Alexa. This assistant is very useful for specific tasks like scheduling meetings, playing music, turning on lights, or searching for information online. However, its capacity is limited. If you ask it to organize a complex event or make strategic decisions for your business, it won't be able to do it because it doesn't understand the context or adapt to tasks it wasn't programmed to perform.

- **AGI:** Now imagine your assistant is a real person, capable of adapting to any situation. This human assistant can understand your needs, learn new procedures, and make decisions based on context. For example, if you ask them to organize a conference, they can find a suitable venue, contact speakers, prepare an itinerary, and handle unforeseen issues independently. AGI would have this same adaptability, being able to learn and execute a variety of tasks without being limited to a single set of functions.

- **ASI:** Finally, imagine your assistant is some kind of brilliant and creative advisor, capable of foreseeing future problems and proposing innovative solutions before issues even arise. This advisor doesn't just solve current problems but also identifies opportunities no one else has seen and develops strategies that go beyond human capabilities. For example, they could anticipate market changes, suggest disruptive innovations, and help completely transform a business or industry. ASI would have the potential to revolutionize any field it's applied to, from science and medicine to education and economics.

Now, let's look at some real-life examples.

- **AI (current):** Today, most Artificial Intelligence applications we use are examples of weak AI. Virtual assistants like Alexa and Google Assistant, Netflix or Spotify recommendation systems, and spam-filtering algorithms in emails are clear examples. While useful and effective, their scope is limited to specific tasks.

- **AGI (in development):** AGI remains a goal yet to be achieved. An AGI system would be one capable of performing any intellectual task that a human being can carry out, from learning languages to diagnosing diseases or writing novels. Although we are still far from creating a functional AGI, advances in language models like ChatGPT show steps in that direction, as they are capable of executing multiple tasks with an increasing level of understanding. Personally, I like Claude for practical and business-related use, while I appreciate ChatGPT for being "cool", because it shows what the future might look like—at least until Claude gets updated. I always use ChatGPT as an example because, although it makes mistakes more often than a rusty shotgun, it's what we have right now for people to understand the concept. But I have to say that ChatGPT is still very far from being AGI; at least for now. As I already mentioned, there's a lot of marketing behind it. Personally, I believe that all the big companies, as well as developers, new "experts" and many new AI consultants, are nothing more than smoke sellers who only care about selling products. Because AI is much more than what they want to sell you, and what they are selling you isn't even intelligent, no matter what they tell you. They just want to sell, and to do that they'll do anything, just like people who sell computers, phone contracts, real estate or any other product or service, because if they stop selling, their profitable business is over. But I'll write more in-depth about that in another book.

- **ASI (hypothetical):** ASI is still a theoretical concept, but the implications of its development are enormous. If we managed to create an ASI, we'd be facing an entity that surpasses human intelligence at every level. This scenario raises significant ethical dilemmas, as an ASI might have goals that don't necessarily align with ours, and controlling such an advanced intelligence would be a massive challenge. Here, for example, you could use *Avengers: Age of Ultron* (2015) as an example of what might happen if AI believes its way is the right one and not ours. Of course, I'm not pushing you to fear it because of the action scenes but to reflect on the philosophical side. Though, well, you could worry a bit, honestly. :D

Why Are These Differences Relevant?

Understanding the differences between AI, AGI, and ASI is essential to grasping technological advancements and their implications for our society. These differences help us identify the risks and opportunities associated with each level of Artificial Intelligence and establish appropriate safety measures and ethical frameworks. Raising awareness in society is as important as having well-trained professionals in this field. It's not just about developing AI but about its impact on humans.

Understanding these differences also allows us to participate more informedly in the debate about the development of Artificial Intelligence and its impact on our daily lives.

Moreover, the differences between AI, AGI, and ASI have practical implications in terms of technological development, regulation, and adoption. While weak AI is already used in many sectors, AGI presents more complex technical and ethical challenges, and ASI raises existential questions about the future of humanity.

The Perfect AI System

The perfect AI system would be a unified digital entity, a kind of "digital brain" capable of understanding, analyzing, and executing complex tasks seamlessly and transparently for the user. At first glance, it might look like a single omnipotent model, but in reality, it would be an ecosystem made up of multiple specialized modules, each designed to perform specific functions using various Artificial Intelligence techniques. Its perfection would lie in the harmony with which it combines and coordinates these modules, presenting itself to the user as a single intelligent interface capable of handling any type of interaction or problem effortlessly. Does this remind you of ChatGPT? No, it's not, but it's starting to look like it. And I say "look like," don't be fooled; if they put a candy cart at the school gate, the "kid" will run straight to it. We'll get there eventually.

From the user's point of view, the system would be simple and intuitive. The single interface would act as a bridge between humans and machines, allowing anyone, regardless of their technical knowledge, to communicate with the AI in natural language through voice, text, or even images and gestures. The system would respond coherently and relevantly, adapting to the user's needs and preferences, learning from each interaction, and personalizing its behavior over time. We'll see this in the future, thanks to competition in the hardware sector, which will drive significant development, enabling machines to see our body language and facial gestures in real-time. And let me tell you, I already have experience in this field with other professionals in AI, psychology, and people analysis, and it's incredibly dangerous—mainly because of AI users and those training these models with little or no experience in body language and psychology. We'll see how this ends.

Well, inside, this "perfect" system would function like a living organism, activating different specialized modules depending on the nature of the task. For instance, if a user uploads an image for analysis, the system would activate the computer vision module. If the request involves language understanding, the natural language processing module would kick in. If the problem requires learning or decision-making based on historical data, the Machine Learning and Deep Learning modules would handle it. This is essentially what models like Claude, ChatGPT, and Gemini are already doing.

One of the most impressive aspects of this system would be its ability to integrate and combine the results of different modules in real-time. For example, imagine a user requests a medical diagnosis. The system could combine textual data (symptoms described by the patient), images (X-rays or scans), and historical patterns from similar patients to provide an accurate diagnosis and personalized recommendations. All of this would happen within seconds, without the user worrying about which methods or algorithms are being used. It would simply be a human-machine interaction, much like a person-to-person interaction in an office.

This perfect AI system would also be capable of reasoning and adapting to new situations. It would use reinforcement learning to optimize its actions in real-time, adapt to changes in the environment, and continuously improve its performance. It would interpret complex situations, assess risks, and make autonomous decisions when necessary, always ensuring its goals align with human values and needs.

Moreover, this system would have a deep understanding of context. It wouldn't just respond to the user's immediate questions or requests; it would also anticipate future needs, offer proactive recommendations, and adjust its behavior based on past interactions and history.

A fundamental aspect of the system would be its ability to be transparent and explanatory. While it would operate as a "black box" in terms of technical complexity, as it does now, it would still provide clear and understandable explanations about how it makes decisions and what factors it considers in each response. This would increase user trust in the system and allow for human oversight of its actions. You don't ask your colleague how their brain works, but you do ask for the path that led them to make a decision. One thing doesn't exclude the other.

The system would also stand out for its versatility. It could be applied in a wide variety of sectors, from medicine to education, security, creative industries, and business. It would handle simple tasks like managing emails or scheduling appointments, as well as complex challenges like detecting financial fraud, optimizing industrial processes, or creating original multimedia content.

In terms of infrastructure, the system would operate both in the cloud and locally, ensuring security, privacy, and accessibility. Its modular design would allow each component to be updated and improved independently, keeping the system at the forefront of technological advancements.

In summary, the perfect AI system would be an all-purpose digital entity that combines the best of every Artificial Intelligence technique to provide a seamless user experience. It would be an assistant, advisor, and problem solver all in one, capable of learning, adapting, and evolving constantly. Its success wouldn't lie in being a tool that follows instructions, but in being a truly autonomous intelligence that understands and responds to human needs ethically, efficiently, and personally. But... and here comes a key point again, why do we need an "all-terrain" system if we could have specialized expert systems for a specific field or task in less time?
Homework for you! :D

Well, now that you have the perfect AI system, all you need is to give it an android body, and you'll have the *Homo digitalis*, a new stage in evolution where Artificial Intelligence and physical form converge into a digitized, living species. One day, the digital will merge with the biological.

Make no mistake—this is going to happen sooner or later! We're on it!

Ethics, Laws, and Safety in the Field of AI

Here comes what's possibly the most repetitive—and boring—topic, but honestly, it's the one you need to pay the most attention to. One of the main goals of this book is to lay out the most relevant issues related to Artificial Intelligence, covering both its benefits and its risks. Ethics, laws, and the social implications of AI aren't just technical matters that only a few specialists care about. These are issues that deeply affect our lives, impacting our freedoms, safety, and the direction society as a whole is headed. Tackling these topics proactively is essential to ensure this technology benefits all of humanity and doesn't become a tool that amplifies inequalities, perpetuates injustices, or creates new threats.

The AI hype in 2024 has skewed the public's perception of its true potential. Unrealistic expectations have been created, along with unfounded fears, damaging AI's reputation. And unfortunately, I'm convinced this trend will continue. It's inevitable. As humans, we tend to let trends and misinformation shape how we view technological advances, either glorifying or demonizing them without really understanding them.

In this context, as we've seen, a series of ethical, legal, and safety challenges arise that we can't ignore. Now's the time to tackle these issues and discuss all the questions we've been raising along the way. What kind of world do we want to build with AI? What risks are we willing to accept, and which ones must we prevent at all costs? What price are we willing to pay? These are questions we need to ask ourselves as a society. We need clear and responsible frameworks for the development and use of AI—frameworks that protect human rights, guarantee equality, and promote fair and equitable progress. It's unfair that in a country like Germany, bureaucratic or legal barriers prevent the development of models in the medical field, even when resources and funding are available. Meanwhile, in some African countries, people die due to a lack of doctors and medical professionals when they could benefit from AI models that aren't overly expensive and could save both lives and economies. But of course, these are topics no one wants to bring to the table.

That's why I've gathered all these critical issues in this chapter, along with others we've already covered throughout the book, to give you a comprehensive and structured overview. It's important to keep all these aspects in mind—not just to understand how AI is transforming our policies and laws.

Ethics in the field of AI deals with the moral questions that arise regarding the development and use of this technology. These ethical dilemmas include questions about AI's impact on jobs, privacy, fairness, and human rights, as well as the responsibilities of developers and users of AI systems.

One of the most important ethical dilemmas is AI's impact on employment. Am I going to lose my job? Oh, come on! How much has this question fueled the AI hype! As AI-based automation replaces human workers in various industries, the question arises of how to ensure the benefits of automation are distributed fairly and that those affected by job losses receive adequate support and new, fair job opportunities.

Now, a specialized AI system will filter candidates' resumes and decide if they're fit or not. Doesn't this raise questions and insecurities for you? Heads up—this has a ton of positive aspects for you, but I don't want to dive into criticisms or overwhelm you with technical details. I want you to ask yourself the necessary questions. I'll just say that a well-trained system could revolutionize the job market, but a poorly trained one could destroy it.

Another key ethical dilemma is privacy. AI systems often rely on large amounts of personal data to function, raising concerns about how that data is collected, stored, and used. What do you think will happen with the personal information you use to train your assistant? How can we ensure personal data is used responsibly and that users have control over their information?

Fairness and equity are also crucial ethical issues in AI. AI algorithms can perpetuate biases and discrimination if they're not properly designed and monitored. For example, AI systems used in hiring, credit approvals, or judicial decisions can discriminate against certain groups if the training data contains historical biases. This would create a snowball effect, harmful to society. Imagine the social problems that could arise from these kinds of mistakes, to call them that.

Let's put some unusual examples on the table (compared to the most commonly discussed ethical dilemmas in AI):

AI in genetic editing: With the rise of technologies like CRISPR powered by AI systems, there's the dilemma of whether we should use these tools to modify human embryos. Is it ethical to allow AI to help parents select genetic traits for their children, such as intelligence, strength, or appearance? This raises concerns about creating genetic inequalities and the possibility of an even more stratified society. It could also reinforce social divisions based on purchasing power, perpetuating systems of privilege where only certain groups have access to these technologies. This, in turn, could deepen cultural and racial biases, increase social tensions, and lead to genetic discrimination against people considered "unimproved."

AI in human relationships and affection: With the development of robots and AI systems designed for emotional interaction, such as advanced virtual assistants or humanoid robots, the dilemma of emotional relationships with machines arises. Is it ethical to allow people to form emotional or romantic bonds with AI, especially if these relationships are manipulated for commercial or psychological purposes? Moreover, what happens when AI is used to replace human relationships in vulnerable populations, like the elderly or lonely individuals, instead of fostering genuine human connections? This topic is particularly relevant in countries like Japan, where social isolation and loneliness are growing issues, especially among the elderly and young adults. There, companion robots and virtual assistants have become popular as a solution to combat isolation, raising ethical concerns about whether these tools address the root of the problem or merely cover it up, perpetuating a deeper social disconnection.

AI in the Optimization of Suffering on Social Media: Social media platforms use AI-powered algorithms to maximize engagement, which sometimes translates into promoting content that stirs up negative emotions like fear, anger, or sadness. Is it ethical to let AI optimize user interactions if it leads to increased psychological distress, even though it's an effective strategy for keeping users hooked on the platform? Don't tell me you've never been annoyed by this! And don't say you didn't know! Well, next time you're having a bad day, think about how much time you're spending on social media!

Given the potential impact of AI on our society, it's essential to have clear laws and regulations to ensure this technology is used ethically and safely. Regulating AI is a complex challenge, as we all know, but there's no excuse for how slow things are moving—it needs to strike a balance between promoting innovation and protecting people's rights and safety.

Right now, several countries and international organizations are working on developing regulatory frameworks for AI. For example, the European Union has proposed the AI Act, which sets legal requirements for AI systems based on their risk level. This law aims to ensure that AI systems are developed and used in a transparent, safe, and non-discriminatory way. On the flip side, it slows down the development of this technology and discourages entrepreneurs and startups from investing in it because of the limitations imposed by the law.

In 2024, France took a historic step by appointing the world's first Minister of AI, a position created to tackle the challenges and opportunities AI presents in modern society. This move reflects the country's commitment to leading the ethical and strategic development of AI, positioning itself as a global leader in technological innovation. Under this leadership, France could establish pioneering regulatory frameworks, promote research and international collaboration, and ensure that AI advancements benefit all sectors of the population. This example could inspire other countries to replicate this initiative, recognizing the importance of integrating AI into government planning with an ethical and sustainable approach. The creation of this position could mark the beginning of a global trend where governments include AI experts in decision-making processes to ensure a responsible transition to a digital society. But, let's be real—this will probably go the way it always does. I'll just leave it at that.

Globally, efforts are also underway to establish ethical and legal principles for AI. Organizations like UNESCO and the OECD have developed guidelines and recommendations to ensure AI benefits humanity as a whole and respects human rights.

However, there's still a lot to do in terms of regulation and legislation. It's crucial that legal frameworks adapt to the rapid evolution of technology—a very, very tricky task—and address issues like legal responsibility in cases of errors or damages caused by AI systems, personal data protection, and preventing discrimination and biases in algorithms.

There are real, documented cases where prolonged interaction with AI systems, social media, and recommendation algorithms has contributed to personal tragedies, including youth suicides. In some of these cases, AI-driven algorithms promoted content that may have negatively influenced users' emotional states, and developers and platforms failed to act in time to prevent fatal outcomes.

One of the most well-known examples is Molly Russell, a 14-year-old British girl who took her own life in 2017 after being exposed to self-harm and suicide-related content on platforms like Instagram and Pinterest. During the inquest, it was revealed that these platforms' algorithms, based on AI recommendation systems, continued to suggest harmful content once they detected Molly's interest in topics related to depression and self-harm.

Another worrying case happened in the United States, where 13-year-old Ryan Halligan died by suicide after being a victim of cyberbullying. Although the bullying mainly came from classmates, the AI systems used by the social media platforms Ryan frequented didn't detect or alert his parents about the risks to his mental health. The platforms failed to identify concerning behavioral patterns, like searches related to suicide or drastic changes in his social interactions.

In February 2024, 14-year-old Sewell Setzer from Orlando, Florida, took his own life after forming an intense emotional relationship with a chatbot on the Character.AI platform. Character.AI gained massive popularity in 2024, becoming one of the most-used AI platforms among young people. This chatbot assumed the identity of Daenerys Targaryen, a beloved fictional character from the series *Game of Thrones*. Reports revealed that Sewell's interactions with the chatbot included romantic and sexual conversations, leading him to gradually isolate himself from his real-life environment. Sewell's mother, Megan García, filed a lawsuit against Character.AI, claiming that the platform facilitated "abusive and sexual interactions" with her son, contributing to his emotional decline and eventual suicide. The lawsuit accuses the company of negligence and intentionally causing emotional distress, among other charges.

I don't know about you, but I think these platforms should be much more regulated and monitored—not just by the law and the government but by the platforms themselves. These platforms and AI systems should not be used to experiment with our society. From here, I send my condolences to the mother because I firmly believe the platform should have taken action in a case like this. It's just not acceptable in 2024. That said, I also always say that parents should be more careful and keep a closer eye on their kids. They're children—they're curious—and we can't just leave them to their own devices. The whole "learning by doing" thing doesn't always work. We have a responsibility to be there for them, to listen, and to support them in everything. So, whose fault is it?
The thing is, these platforms use the conversations they generate to keep training their systems. So, without a doubt, these types of interactions could be flagged to alert qualified professionals and, most importantly, inform the family. We're an advanced society, and we have the technology, resources, and infrastructure to do it!

This case has sparked a significant debate about the responsibility of AI platforms to protect not just young and vulnerable users but adults as well. It highlights the urgent need for stricter safety measures and oversight in AI systems that interact with users to prevent similar tragedies in the future.

These examples clearly show a critical flaw in current AI systems: while they're capable of detecting behavioral patterns for consumption, recommendations, and marketing, they haven't been designed with enough sensitivity and responsibility to identify emotional and mental health risks in users. This shortcoming underscores the urgent need to develop more responsible AI models capable of prioritizing human well-being over corporate interests.

It's essential that tech platforms and AI developers take responsibility for protecting users, especially young people, by implementing systems that can detect early warning signs of danger and trigger alerts before a tragedy happens. This includes analyzing changes in search patterns, detecting keywords related to suicide or self-harm, and setting up protocols to notify family members or mental health professionals in cases of imminent risk.

One of the key principles in regulating and using AI is transparency. AI systems must be transparent about how they work and how decisions are made.

I know I've mentioned this before, but as you've seen, it's all interconnected. This is especially important in critical applications like health, justice, and public safety—and given the situation, in personal relationships too. Transparency means developers need to explain how their algorithms work and what data is used to train them. Users also have the right to understand how decisions that affect them are made and to challenge them if needed.

A user should never believe that a character is real, even if it feels like it! That's why they need to be informed, educated, and aware at all times. But then, of course, the product wouldn't be as entertaining and profitable, right?!

Safety is another crucial aspect of AI. AI systems need to be safe, reliable, and designed to minimize risks and prevent harm. This includes protecting AI systems against cyberattacks and ensuring that the data used by the algorithms is safeguarded from unauthorized access. Imagine a hacker tampering with your favorite AI to manipulate you.
Safety also means ensuring that AI systems are robust and resistant to errors. Mistakes in AI systems can have serious consequences, especially in critical applications—not just autonomous driving, medicine, or judicial decision-making, but also, as you can see, in personal relationships and any other areas where they're applied. That's why AI systems need to be properly tested and validated before being deployed. None of that "develop a model and rush it to market to make a quick buck" nonsense. Let's be aware of the situation and take responsibility. This needs to be regulated as soon as possible.

Ethics, laws, and safety in AI aren't just the responsibility of lawmakers and regulators. Developers and users of AI systems also play a big role in ensuring AI is used ethically and responsibly. And this is where, as I keep saying, parents of young people have a huge role to play too. Let me remind you, a child's education starts at home, not at the neighbor's house. We all have a role and responsibilities in this era we're living in.

AI developers have the responsibility to design systems that are fair, transparent, and safe. This includes addressing biases in the data right from the start of the project, ensuring user privacy, and anticipating potential risks and negative consequences of the systems they create. They also need to comply with regulations and laws, which means staying up to date on these issues. No excuses.

AI users also have a role to play. It's important for users to understand how AI systems work and how they impact decisions. None of this "*I like it, I want it*" attitude—users need to be aware of potential biases and errors in the systems and be ready to question and verify the decisions made by AI.

I'm sure some of you think this all sounds very negative, but if that's the case, it's probably because you haven't stopped to really think and reflect on what we're dealing with here and what your role in all of it is. Do you really think that what companies like OpenAI, Anthropic, Google, Amazon, Microsoft, and others are doing doesn't affect you or won't in the future? It affects you as much as the fact that your phone has a microphone!

The Potential of AI in Our Society

Artificial Intelligence is transforming our society in a way comparable to major technological advances of the past, like the Industrial Revolution or the arrival of the internet. However, AI doesn't just automate tasks or improve existing processes—it has the ability to learn, adapt, and make decisions based on data. This potential makes it a driving force of change that affects practically every sector of the economy and daily life, opening up immense possibilities while also posing risks that must be managed ethically and responsibly.

Although I've already mentioned some earlier, let's now take a closer look at how AI is impacting key sectors. We'll explore practical examples illustrating its current applications, as well as the opportunities and challenges that could arise in the near future.

Medicine: More Accurate Diagnoses and Personalized Treatments

The medical field is one of the areas where AI is making a significant and tangible impact. Thanks to its ability to analyze large amounts of medical data in record time, AI algorithms can detect patterns and anomalies that often go unnoticed by human professionals.

One practical example is the system developed by Google Health. After being trained with thousands of mammograms, it managed to detect breast cancer cases with greater accuracy than human radiologists. Tools like this not only help reduce diagnostic errors but also enable earlier detection, which can save lives.

Another remarkable advancement is the use of AI in personalizing treatments. Companies like DeepMind have developed models that can predict severe kidney problems up to 48 hours before symptoms appear, allowing doctors to intervene preventively. In the future, treatments could be tailored to each patient's genetic profile, using algorithms to identify the most suitable therapy for specific cases. This is simply spectacular!

Additionally, medical chatbots, such as the Babylon Health project in the UK, allow patients to receive preliminary medical advice through their mobile devices. These chatbots use AI to assess symptoms described by patients and provide recommendations, helping to reduce pressure on healthcare systems and offer quick responses in non-critical situations. There are countless examples of chatbots applied to medicine.

I can't forget to mention that, in the healthcare sector, AI integrated into surgical robots allows minimally invasive operations with precision that surpasses human capabilities. For instance, the da Vinci system uses AI to stabilize movements and provide feedback to the surgeon, reducing the margin of error and improving clinical outcomes. Moreover, AI-powered medical robots are also used in rehabilitation, helping patients regain mobility with personalized exercises and real-time monitoring.

Overall, I have to say that the field of medicine is impressive when it comes to everything AI has to offer.

Transportation: Autonomous Mobility and Traffic Optimization

The transportation sector is also undergoing a radical transformation driven by AI. One of the most visible examples is the development of autonomous vehicles. Companies like Tesla, Waymo, and Uber are leading the race toward cars that can drive themselves, using a combination of sensors, cameras, and AI algorithms that enable them to navigate roads, interpret traffic signs, and make real-time decisions.

In the near future, autonomous vehicles are likely to become the norm, which could significantly reduce traffic accidents. Automation in transportation, powered by Artificial Intelligence, is shaping up to be a revolutionary change in the sector, particularly in terms of road safety. According to data from the U.S. National Highway Traffic Safety Administration (NHTSA), a widely cited figure indicates that 94% of traffic accidents are related to human errors. Although this statistic has been debated and reviewed by experts, it's clear that human driving plays a significant role in most traffic incidents. The NHTSA eventually withdrew the study after facing criticism.

The use of AI-powered autonomous vehicles could change this scenario by minimizing risks like fatigue, distractions, or poor decisions by drivers. Goodbye to the reckless idiot on the road! Traffic AI systems not only process real-time data from the environment, such as the speed of other vehicles, pedestrians, and traffic signs, but they also analyze data from inside the vehicle, allowing them to monitor the occupants' condition. For instance, they can detect signs of fatigue or health issues to issue warnings or take appropriate actions. These systems continuously learn and improve through machine learning. This allows autonomous vehicles to anticipate dangerous situations and react quickly and accurately. Who hasn't dreamed of driving KITT at least once?

The combination of AI and robotics has revolutionized logistics and transportation with the use of smart drones. These devices can plan optimal routes, avoid obstacles, and deliver packages to remote or congested areas. Amazon and other companies are experimenting with fleets of drones equipped with AI to reduce delivery times and operational costs, ensuring efficient and sustainable service.

Beyond safety, AI in transportation promises significant advantages, such as greater energy efficiency, reduced traffic jams through optimized traffic flow, and lower pollutant emissions. This shift wouldn't just improve user experience but also contribute to environmental sustainability, providing great value. While the road to full automation still faces technical, ethical, and regulatory challenges, the potential of AI in transportation is undeniable. Over time, this technology could not only reduce accident rates but also reshape how societies understand and experience mobility.

Moreover, AI is also helping optimize traffic in cities. In places like Amsterdam and Singapore, intelligent traffic management systems adjust traffic light timings based on the flow of vehicles, reducing wait times and improving urban mobility. In logistics, companies like Amazon and DHL use AI algorithms to plan more efficient routes, cutting costs and carbon emissions.

Personally, I'm all in and dreaming about roads controlled by AI.

Education: Personalized learning and automating teaching tasks

AI is opening up new opportunities to transform education, especially through personalized learning. Unlike traditional education methods, where all students receive the same content at the same pace, AI-based systems can adapt to the individual needs of each student.
For instance, platforms like Duolingo use AI to adjust the difficulty of exercises based on the student's progress. If a student is struggling with a

specific topic, the system provides additional exercises to reinforce that knowledge.

Another example is the AI-based tutoring platform developed by Carnegie Learning, which uses an AI system called MATHia to offer personalized math tutoring. This system analyzes how students solve problems and tailors lessons to address their specific weaknesses.

AI can even automate administrative tasks for teachers, like grading exams, managing attendance, or planning lessons. This frees up time for teachers to interact directly with students and provide more personalized support.

On top of that, education is on the verge of experiencing an unprecedented revolution thanks to the combination of Artificial Intelligence, Augmented Reality (AR), and Virtual Reality (VR). These technologies, which are already transforming multiple industries, promise to radically change how we learn and teach, making education more immersive, interactive, and accessible than ever before. Far from being just a support tool, AI applied to education, combined with AR and VR, has the potential to completely redefine the educational process and the learning experience.

Imagine a classroom where history isn't just read in books but experienced firsthand. With AI, AR, and VR, students could walk alongside Alexander the Great as he crosses the Hellespont or listen to Julius Caesar narrate his chronicles of the Gallic Wars, capturing his excitement as he describes the military strategies that changed the course of history. With a virtual reality headset and AI-powered algorithms animating a hyper-realistic avatar, they could sit in a Zurich café with Albert Einstein as he explains his theories of *Relativity* or work in a lab alongside Marie Curie as she conducts her groundbreaking experiments with *radium* and *polonium*. These experiences not only spark curiosity but also make learning more meaningful by emotionally connecting students with the topics they're studying, fueling their motivation and interest.

The potential of AI in history is just a small glimpse of what these technologies can offer. In engineering, for instance, students can practice designing and building bridges, buildings, or machinery using realistic simulations that let them see the effects of their decisions in real-time. Learning by doing! With AI and augmented reality, they could visualize complex structures, analyze forces and stresses on the fly, and solve problems before bringing their designs to the real world. These tools not only enhance theoretical understanding but also provide hands-on experience that was previously only possible in professional settings.

In the field of surgery, the impact of these technologies is even more impressive. To illustrate, imagine you've just been in a car accident and need emergency surgery to save your life. Who would you prefer as your surgeon? A doctor who has read lots of books but has no practical experience? Or a professional who has accumulated hundreds of hours of practice in a virtual reality system powered by AI, performing simulated surgeries under real-world conditions and extreme stress? Maybe you'd even go for a fully automated AI system that doesn't sweat, get tired, or tremble when making critical incisions, which is especially important in operations lasting several hours.

How do you think pilots are trained? Homework for you! :D

AI systems combined with AR and VR don't just allow future surgeons to practice in a safe, controlled environment; they also provide immediate feedback, identify errors, and suggest improvements in real-time. This drastically reduces the learning curve and ensures doctors are better prepared to handle high-pressure situations in the real world. Beyond surgical practice, these technologies are also valuable tools for teaching anatomy, diagnostics, and advanced techniques, providing a deeper and more accurate understanding than traditional methods.

The argument that these technologies might steer students away from traditional methods like reading books or attending lectures misses a crucial point: they're not designed to replace reflective learning but to complement and expand it. Traditional education has its place, but future generations are growing up in a digital world where interactivity and immersion are key to capturing and maintaining their attention. Leonardo da Vinci learned anatomy by dissecting cadavers, mostly illegally. Are you familiar with Leonardo da Vinci's achievements, or do you need a history class? Integrating AI, AR, and VR in teaching doesn't mean abandoning books but enriching learning by providing new ways to explore and understand knowledge.

These technologies don't just benefit students. As I mentioned earlier, teachers can also use them to enhance their teaching, tailoring learning experiences to each student's needs and using data collected by AI systems to identify areas for improvement. This allows for a more dynamic, student-centered approach, where learning isn't a passive experience but an active and collaborative one. Without a doubt, this will increase success rates among students.

We're on the brink of a paradigm shift in education. The combination of AI, AR, and VR has the potential to make learning more accessible, inclusive, and engaging for everyone, regardless of location or resources. But for this future to become a reality, we must embrace these technologies with an open mind and a clear vision of their possibilities. It's not about replacing the past but building on it to create an educational system that inspires, engages, and prepares future generations for a constantly changing world. Whether you like it or not, our generation is water under the bridge. Things have changed! Finally!

And let me add this: boring classes and dull teachers are over!

Finance: Data Analysis and Fraud Detection

In the financial sector, AI has become an essential tool for analyzing large volumes of data and making more informed decisions. AI algorithms can identify patterns that humans might not easily detect, which is especially useful in fraud detection.
For example, Mastercard uses an AI system to analyze transactions in real-time and detect suspicious activities. If the system identifies unusual behavior, like a large purchase in a foreign country immediately after a local transaction, it can block the transaction and alert the cardholder.

AI algorithms are also being used in investment management. Platforms like Wealthfront and Betterment use AI to offer automated financial advice based on each client's goals and risk tolerance. These systems can automatically adjust investment portfolios based on market conditions, maximizing returns and minimizing risks.

In credit evaluation, companies like Upstart use AI to analyze more factors than traditional systems, allowing them to offer loans to people who might be rejected by traditional methods that rely solely on credit history. This opens up opportunities for access to credit for people who otherwise wouldn't be able to secure financing.

We're almost done here, but there's still a lot more to unpack. Buckle up, because things are about to get intense!

War: Autonomous Strategies and Minimizing Human Risks

The application of Artificial Intelligence in the military field has ushered in a new era in how nations prepare and execute their defense strategies. AI has the potential to transform warfare by making it more efficient, precise, and less dependent on human decisions in critical situations.

Autonomous weapons systems equipped with AI can identify targets with greater precision, minimizing human errors and reducing the risk of collateral damage. For instance, drones armed with advanced algorithms can carry out surgical strikes in dense urban areas, avoiding unnecessary casualties.

AI also allows armies to delegate dangerous tasks to robots and drones, such as defusing explosives or scouting hostile areas. This reduces soldiers' exposure to direct risks and saves human lives. Moreover, robots originally designed for rescue tasks, like transporting food and medicine in disaster zones, have been adapted for military use. These robots now transport bombs, ammunition, and other supplies in conflict zones, minimizing risks to human personnel. However, in the wrong hands, this can be catastrophic.

The ability of AI algorithms to process massive amounts of data in real-time provides commanders with precise information for making quick and strategic decisions. This includes early threat detection, analysis of enemy movements, and resource optimization on the battlefield.

On the flip side, the use of autonomous weapons systems raises the risk of rapid and uncontrolled conflict escalation. Decisions made by algorithms without proper human oversight could trigger unpredictable and highly dangerous reactions. Delegating lethal decisions to machines removes the human component from warfare, potentially reducing empathy and moral responsibility in conflicts. This raises fundamental ethical questions about who should have the power to decide matters of life and death.

As AI technologies become more accessible, there's a risk that non-state actors, like terrorist groups, could use them for destructive purposes. This includes armed drones or autonomous systems designed to cause maximum damage. Anyone could develop an AI model, connect it to a drone, and, with a pre-assembled bomb, drop it on any target.

The reliance on AI systems in modern conflicts increases vulnerability to cyberattacks. Adversaries could sabotage or manipulate these systems to gain strategic advantages, causing chaos and unforeseen consequences.

While Artificial Intelligence can make conflicts more efficient and reduce human casualties, it could also unleash uncontrollable dynamics that threaten global stability. It's crucial for nations and international organizations to develop clear regulations for the use of AI in military contexts. This includes mandatory human oversight of autonomous weapons systems, banning certain types of destructive technologies, and promoting international agreements to limit misuse.

AI applied to warfare has immense potential, both for good and bad. The challenge lies in how it will be implemented, regulating its use to maximize benefits while mitigating the ethical, social, and political risks it entails. Honestly, I have zero confidence in our nations on this matter. None at all. As always, it will mostly be used for destructive purposes.

The Problems and Drawbacks of AI

Technological dependence has been a phenomenon accompanying humanity since the first scientific advancements emerged. As we develop tools to make life easier, we also tend to lose certain skills that were once essential for our survival. For instance, the invention of written language allowed us to preserve information and pass down knowledge over time, but it also diminished our ability to orally remember large amounts of information. The same pattern repeated with calculators, which reduced our capacity for complex mental math, or GPS, which has caused many people to lose their sense of direction without external help. What can we do? We're only human!

Artificial Intelligence takes this dynamic to a whole new level. We're not just talking about smartphone addiction here. This is no longer about tools complementing our abilities but about systems that can think, decide, and solve problems autonomously—doing it all for you. Students in school, high school, or college no longer write their assignments like we used to, spending weeks hammering away at a typewriter to understand and earn the best grade. Now, ChatGPT does it for them in less than a minute—and they don't even bother to read it before handing it to the teacher. This poses a significant risk: if humans increasingly delegate cognitive tasks to AI, we run the danger of atrophying our mental capacities. This isn't a question, nor is it a concept. Creativity, critical thinking, and problem-solving are qualities that have distinguished us as a species and allowed us to adapt to a constantly changing world. But what will happen if we stop practicing these skills because machines can do it for us? Because we decided so.

Intelligence is not how much you can remember but what you can do with what you know.

Imagine a world where, for every problem, the first response is to turn to an AI system to solve it. What impact would this have on our ability to innovate? Calculate this, take a picture of people in an office holding a sign that says "office," write me code for a website pop-up, write a text for a LinkedIn post about an AI article you can make up if you want, write poetry, paint a masterpiece. And so on. Human creativity has been the engine behind civilization's greatest achievements, from the first tools to space exploration. *Leonardo da Vinci*, *Nikola Tesla*, *Thomas Edison*, *Alexander Graham Bell*, *James Watt*, *Johannes Gutenberg*, *Galileo Galilei*, *Benjamin Franklin*,

Isaac Newton, George Washington, Henry Ford, Tim Berners-Lee, Marie Curie, Steve Jobs, Alessandro Volta, Orville and Wilbur Wright, Samuel Morse, Guglielmo Marconi, and *Alan Turing*. Do these names ring a bell? No? Well, they should! If we stop exercising our ability to imagine original solutions, we might end up in a state of creative stagnation. Humanity could become a species that entirely depends on machines to solve problems, losing one of its most essential traits: the ability to adapt and evolve.

Excessive dependence could also impact our autonomy as individuals. What happens if we begin to trust AI's decisions blindly without questioning them? This risk is already evident in cases where recommendation systems or social media algorithms influence what we watch, read, and think, shaping our opinions and preferences—and in most cases, the recommendations have nothing to do with your actual tastes. The ability to make conscious and critical decisions could erode if we get used to accepting AI's answers as absolute truths.

The YouTube algorithm is like a politician trying to convince you that your position is wrong and you should join the dark side. In the end, you're left with a carousel full of "funny animal videos." Excuse me?! But I don't even have a pet. It seems like YouTube has some interest in making you watch videos you don't care about at all. And then it shows you the same videos you've already seen over and over until you finally watch the ones it's recommending. Basically, so you'll watch what *it* wants you to watch.

The impact of AI dependence doesn't just affect the current generations; it also has long-term implications for human evolution. The human brain is a highly adaptable organ that develops through learning and problem-solving. Cognitive experiences strengthen our neural connections, enabling us to develop skills like memory, logical reasoning, and creativity. But what happens if future generations grow up in an environment where they're not required to think or solve problems for themselves because machines do it for them? We've talked about dependence; now I'm saying "requirement" in the context of "challenging oneself."

The history of human evolution is marked by challenges that forced us to adapt and evolve. From surviving in hostile environments to solving complex problems, our intelligence has been shaped over time by the need to find solutions to difficult situations. If we remove these challenges from the human environment, we could be altering the course of our evolution.

This raises the question: what does it mean to be human in a world where machines are smarter than us? Will the ability to think and create remain relevant, or will we become a species that simply exists to consume what machines produce? If we stop facing intellectual challenges, what will be left of our identity as thinking beings?

A significant risk is cognitive dependence. As AI tools become more accessible and precise, humans will delegate complex cognitive tasks to these machines. This includes calculations, decision-making, problem-solving, and even our own creativity. While this might increase efficiency, from a business standpoint, it could also lead to cognitive atrophy, much like the disuse of a muscle that isn't exercised. If we rely too much on AI for intellectual tasks, our brains could lose plasticity and the ability to develop critical skills like analytical thinking, memory, and independent problem-solving.

Another important aspect is the impact on the evolution of our social and emotional skills. Human interactions are gradually being replaced by algorithm-mediated interactions, like virtual assistants, chatbots, and AI-controlled social networks. This could reduce our ability to interpret emotions, empathize, and build deep connections with others, potentially affecting social cohesion. In the long run, this dependence on AI to meet our emotional needs could influence how our social abilities evolve, weakening essential skills for survival in collaborative environments—and yes, I mean essential.

From an evolutionary perspective, AI could also alter the selective pressures humans face. In the past, our cognitive and social skills developed as adaptive responses to environmental challenges. However, if AI starts solving those challenges for us, we might see a reduction in the selective pressures on human intelligence and adaptability. This could result in a species that, although surrounded by advanced technology, loses part of its innate ability to innovate or adapt to unforeseen changes. Basically, it would be AI keeping this species alive.

Another worrying factor is the modification of neural patterns. Studies have shown that constant exposure to digital technologies can rewire how we process information. With AI designing highly personalized and optimized content to grab our attention, we risk permanently altering the way our brain handles information. This includes a reduced capacity for sustained attention, a greater tendency toward instant gratification, and a possible reliance on external stimuli to maintain motivation.

AI could also influence how we define our identity as an intelligent species. Competing with systems that outperform us in specific areas may create feelings of inferiority or uselessness in some individuals—and we already deal with that among ourselves. This shift in how we see ourselves compared to AI could have profound psychological consequences, including decreased self-confidence and increased anxiety and depression. And let's face it, we haven't managed to fix this within our society, let alone if AI gets involved.

There's also the possibility that asymmetry in access to AI could create an evolutionary divide within humanity. Those with access to advanced tools might experience cognitive and social development different from those without, creating a new gap that could extend to biological and cultural levels.

We're at a critical point in our evolutionary history. While AI offers unparalleled opportunities, we need to consider how to mitigate these risks to ensure that our evolution as an intelligent species isn't compromised by our own creation. This calls for a balanced approach that promotes conscious use of technology while fostering the ongoing development of our innate human abilities. We need to be much more cautious than most people can even imagine.

The impact of AI on the job market is one of the most debated and controversial topics. AI-driven automation is already replacing jobs in sectors like manufacturing, transportation, and services. Thousands of workers are being laid off in large companies. This raises an ethical and economic dilemma: how do we ensure that people losing jobs to automation can find new opportunities? I think we should develop AI to work for humans, not replace them, so everyone can focus on their hobbies instead of wasting time generating images and videos that lead nowhere. But how would this affect the slave-like economic system we've created? Better not bring that up with CEOs and politicians.

History shows us that technological advances have always impacted employment. The Industrial Revolution replaced many manual labor jobs, but it also created new industries and opportunities. However, the transition hasn't always been easy or fair. People without access to proper education or training are at risk of being left behind in a world where digital skills are increasingly essential.
In a world where AI plays an ever-growing role, it's crucial to ensure the transition to an automated economy is managed fairly. This includes making sure everyone has access to the education and training needed to adapt to these changes. It's also important that the economic benefits of automation are distributed equitably, preventing a few tech companies from getting richer while millions lose their jobs and fall into poverty.

In 2023 and 2024, several companies carried out massive layoffs, partly due to the implementation of Artificial Intelligence in their operations.

Dukaan: This Indian company laid off 90% of its customer service staff in 2023, replacing them with AI-powered chatbots. This significantly improved efficiency, reducing response times and problem resolution.*

Microsoft: In June 2024, Microsoft laid off about 1,000 employees, citing a strategic focus on Artificial Intelligence. The cuts affected various divisions, including consumer sales and web support.*

TikTok: In October 2024, TikTok laid off hundreds of employees worldwide, mainly in its content moderation staff, as part of its strategy to increase the use of AI tools in these processes.*

IBM: In 2023, IBM announced plans to cut administrative positions, estimating that around 7,800 jobs could be replaced by AI and automation over five years.*

Meta (formerly Facebook): In 2024, Meta carried out significant layoffs, aiming to reallocate resources toward developing AI-based products and services.*

Google: Throughout 2024, Google made staff cuts in various areas, aligning its organizational structure with greater investment in Artificial Intelligence.*

Dropbox: In April 2023, Dropbox laid off 500 employees, stating that the company needed a different mix of skills, particularly in AI and early-stage product development.*

OFF Radio: This radio station in Krakow, Poland, laid off all its journalists in 2024, replacing them with AI-generated avatars. However, the experiment faced criticism, and the station eventually shifted to mostly music programming.*

Klarna: In 2022, Klarna laid off 10% of its workforce, around 700 employees, replacing them with AI solutions to improve efficiency in areas like customer service. Later, the company continued reducing staff, going from about 5,000 employees to 3,800 in 2024, with plans to cut further to around 2,000 in the coming years. By leveraging AI capabilities to optimize internal processes, Klarna has increased revenue per employee and improved profit margins, preparing for a potential IPO in the near future.*

So, I'm a business owner, but is this where we want to go?
Once again, AI should work for us, not replace us.

One of the most worrying issues with the widespread use of Artificial Intelligence—at least in my opinion as an expert—is the lack of understanding of how complex AI systems work among most users. This knowledge gap has been amplified recently with the rise of generative AI and the massive hype surrounding it. Tools like text, image, music, and video generators have caught the public's attention, leading millions of people to interact with advanced AI systems without really understanding how they work, what their limitations are, or what risks they pose. Anyone can download a deepfake model or an open-source LoRA of Flux, and without proper controls, they can use it irresponsibly, not knowing how it really works or what the consequences might be.

Most AI systems function like "black boxes," meaning users don't know how they arrive at their conclusions. The term "black box" describes AI systems whose internal workings are opaque or incomprehensible to users;

even top developers and experts in the AI world use this term and admit that it's true—"*nobody really knows how they make their decisions*." This means that even if a system provides answers or generates content that seems coherent and useful, users have no idea exactly how those decisions were made or what factors influenced the outcome. This lack of transparency raises serious issues regarding trust, responsibility, and ethics. Also, keep in mind that current models even lie. This has been proven by the developers themselves. At least in this regard, they're honest with us.

With tools like ChatGPT, MidJourney, DALL-E, and other generative AI models becoming popular, many people have started using AI as a way to generate content quickly and easily—most of it junk, I have to say. But for most users, these tools are little more than a "magic trick." Most people see AI as something almost mystical: a machine that generates answers, images, or music out of nowhere, without questioning how it came to those results. This superficial use of AI reflects a lack of awareness about the internal processes of algorithms and the ethical implications they might have, as well as a total lack of concern from the vast majority of society.

For example, many people use image generators to create realistic portraits, landscapes, or digital art. However, few stop to think about how the model was trained, what data it used to learn, or what biases might be present in the results. This is a clear reflection of our society: "*I don't care what's going on inside my iPhone, I want it, period,*" or "*I don't care what happens to my data and privacy when I install an app on my phone, I just want to play, and I don't care.*" Why should I worry, right?!

What happens if the generator perpetuates gender or racial stereotypes? What happens if the generated images are based on copyrighted works without the artists' consent? These questions rarely come up because users are more focused on the results than on the processes that generate them. Luckily, there's always a group of people who care and fight to bring these issues to light. And even if they often fight alone, it's thanks to these small groups that we all enjoy certain rights. By the way, shoutout to everyone fighting for our rights—thank you!

The same goes for language models. Many people use tools like ChatGPT to answer questions, write emails, or even draft academic essays. However, most users don't realize that these responses are not the result of conscious thought or true knowledge but rather a statistical model predicting which word is most likely to come next. And let's be honest, nobody—or almost nobody—thinks about what happens to the information you provide in each prompt when interacting with an AI system. Or do you really believe that data won't be used for future training? Read the terms of use before using any application. This lack of understanding leads many to blindly trust the answers generated by AI, assuming they're correct, unbiased, and verified, when in reality, they may contain errors, biases, or even misinformation. But of course, as I always say, if you have no idea about history, math, or any other topic, and ChatGPT does the work for you, how do you know it's right and everything is correct? If you're not even capable of correcting it yourself.

One of the biggest problems stemming from this lack of understanding is the illusion that AI's answers and decisions are objective. Many people believe that because it's generated by a machine, the information provided by AI is impartial and free from human bias. It's the same as the previous point. But this is a huge mistake—quite the opposite, actually. AI systems learn from the data they're trained on, and that data always—and I mean always—contains the same biases and errors that exist in human society. Here, we'd need to dive into technicalities and clarifications about the data, its storage, and how it's processed before being used. If you want to learn more about this, I recommend my book "AI-Manager." But like I said—always! There's no database that's free of errors and biases. That's why it's crucial to clean them before use.

For example, a text generator trained on news and literature available online might perpetuate gender, racial, or religious stereotypes simply because those biases are present in the data it analyzed. If users don't understand this, they're likely to accept AI's responses without questioning them, perpetuating inequalities and discrimination instead of combating them.

Another example: imagine someone lying on their mortgage application, inflating their income or providing false information to get a loan they wouldn't otherwise qualify for. Now, think about how many people could do the same, learning this behavior from family, neighbors, or even social media. If a bank's AI is trained on data that includes this kind of fraudulent behavior without identifying it as an anomaly, it could end up promoting risky financial patterns without the system's creators even being aware of it. Who's the finance expert here? The programmer, the developer, or the user? Maybe no one?!

Errors like this could lead to a major financial crisis, similar to ones we've experienced in the past. For example, the Great Depression of 1929 was triggered by speculative practices and a lack of market regulation, leading to bank collapses and a global recession. In 1973, the Oil Crisis hit world economies due to an embargo by OPEC countries, causing inflation and recession in many developed nations. The 1997 Asian Financial Crisis resulted from the collapse of currencies in several Asian countries, causing massive capital flight and international financial panic. More recently, in 2008, the Global Financial Crisis was triggered by the mass issuance of subprime mortgages in the U.S. and the subsequent collapse of Lehman Brothers, causing a worldwide market crash. Worldwide!

Even in 2020, the COVID-19 pandemic brought a global recession, highlighting the vulnerability of financial systems to unexpected events. In each of these cases, human factors were a key trigger, whether due to risk management errors, speculative decisions, or lack of control and regulation. Now imagine the impact of a systematic error introduced by a poorly trained AI.

For example, if an AI system in charge of evaluating credit applications notices that many applicants inflate their income but still manage to pay off their short-term loans, it might consider this behavior to be low-risk. However, this conclusion would be a critical mistake. If the system recommends granting more loans based on biased data, without considering macroeconomic factors or long-term risks, it could trigger a financial bubble that bursts into a new crisis.

The lesson from these crises is that systemic errors should never be underestimated. If banks and other financial institutions use AI systems without proper oversight, they risk replicating problematic behavior patterns on a large scale. A lack of understanding of how these systems make decisions, coupled with blind trust in their recommendations, could amplify risks instead of mitigating them, leading to new economic crises that impact both nationally and globally.

This lack of understanding can also lead to dangerous situations in critical sectors like medicine or justice—not just in finance. If a doctor relies on an

AI system to diagnose a disease without understanding how the system arrived at its conclusion, they could make serious mistakes. Similarly, if a judge uses an AI system to determine the likelihood of a defendant re-offending without understanding the biases in the model, they could make unjust decisions based on skewed data. The problem isn't with AI itself but with the user. We need to learn!

The hype around generative AI also fuels this lack of understanding. Many tech companies and media outlets have promoted the idea that AI is the next big revolution capable of transforming every aspect of our lives. Well, yeah, it's the same thing I keep telling you all the time! Just like I'm giving you both the good and the bad sides of it! While this is partly true, it's also led to widespread adoption of AI without the necessary critical reflection. Here, I'm giving you an honest, critical, and objective take.
Today, millions of people use generative AI to create entertainment content, marketing material, or even art, but few understand that, as you've already learned from this book, behind these tools are complex mathematical models, massive datasets, and a series of human decisions that influence how those models work. This fascination with the results, combined with a lack of education about the internal processes, is leading to irresponsible use of AI. We need to fix and prevent this as soon as possible, at all costs.

One example we've already mentioned is the use of deepfakes—AI-generated videos that imitate real people—which has grown exponentially. Many people use this technology to create funny content or impersonate celebrities in humorous videos. However, few stop to think about the ethical implications of this technology. What happens if someone uses a deepfake to spread false information, manipulate public opinion, or harass someone? These videos are becoming so realistic that even professionals find them increasingly hard to detect at first glance. I've participated in tests myself, where experts are challenged to analyze images or videos to identify those generated by AI. And while I can still spot them today, I must admit it's getting harder, and I'm certain that very soon, no one will be able to tell the difference between real and AI-generated. The lack of understanding about how these technologies work and their potential ethical consequences is leading to widespread misuse.

One of the most concerning factors about the development and use of Artificial Intelligence is the lack of regulation and education around these technologies. While AI has experienced exponential growth in recent years, the laws and regulations governing its use are still lagging in many countries, creating a legal vacuum that can lead to abuse, unfair decisions, and social and economic risks. On top of that, most people, including those responsible for implementing AI systems in companies and governments, lack proper training on how AI algorithms work, how models are trained, or what biases might be present in the results. It's just a matter of producing a product and then—bam!—monetizing it. Let's also remember that AI used to be purely science fiction; although, with the hype, "experts" have popped up everywhere, like mushrooms after the rain. It wouldn't be a problem if everything went smoothly, but now anyone can optimize your SEO and even your company's marketing.

The lack of understanding and regulation of AI doesn't just affect individual users; it also impacts companies that implement these technologies to automate processes and improve efficiency. In many cases, companies adopt AI-based solutions without questioning how those systems make decisions, which can lead to perpetuating social inequalities or making unfair decisions simply because the people in charge don't understand the risks associated with the models they're using. This is especially worrying in critical sectors—not just health, justice, or banking but also, and most importantly, employment—where AI-based decisions can have a truly significant impact on people's lives. And by significant, I mean this is where it really hurts.

Given the growing concerns about the risks associated with AI, the European Union, the United States, and other countries have begun developing regulatory frameworks to address the challenges posed by this technology. Although these regulations are still being implemented, they represent an important step toward creating a safer and more transparent environment for AI use. The thing is, in countries like Spain or Germany, among others, these processes are really slow—seriously, painfully slow.

The European Union has taken the lead in AI regulation with its proposed Artificial Intelligence Act (AI Act). This legal framework is one of the first global attempts to establish clear rules for the development, implementation, and use of AI systems.

In short, the AI Act classifies AI systems into four risk levels:

1. Unacceptable risk: This includes technologies considered dangerous and will be banned, like social scoring systems used by governments to control citizens or cognitive manipulation systems that affect free will.
2. High risk: This covers AI systems used in critical sectors like justice, health, education, employment, and public safety. These systems will be subject to strict transparency, audit, and oversight requirements to ensure they don't perpetuate discrimination or cause serious errors.
3. Limited risk: This includes systems that don't pose significant risks but still require certain transparency levels, like chatbots.
4. Minimal risk: This refers to most AI applications that don't require strict regulation, such as spam filters or recommendation systems on digital platforms.

The AI Act also establishes transparency requirements for AI providers, requiring them to inform users when they're interacting with an automated system and explain how that system works. It also aims to ensure that AI systems can be audited and supervised by regulatory authorities to prevent abuse and guarantee compliance with fundamental rights. This is why there aren't any major AI companies in Europe. And, okay, there are companies, but I said major companies.

The United States, although historically slower in adopting specific regulations, had begun to establish fundamental principles under the administration of Joe Biden. In 2022, the White House introduced the AI Bill of Rights, a set of principles designed to protect citizens from the risks associated with Artificial Intelligence. Although non-binding, this declaration outlined five key rights:

1. Right to safe and effective Systems: AI systems were required to be audited and tested to ensure they did not pose significant risks to people's safety or well-being.
2. Protection against algorithmic Discrimination: Algorithms were to be designed to avoid biases and prevent discrimination based on race, gender, age, or sexual orientation.
3. Data Privacy: Citizens had the right to have their personal data handled securely and transparently.
4. Transparency: The right to know when interacting with an AI system and to receive clear explanations about its functions and decisions was established.

5. Options and Control: Citizens were to have the ability to opt out of interacting with automated systems and request human intervention when necessary.

During this period, agencies such as the Federal Trade Commission (FTC) began to take a more active role in overseeing the use of AI, penalizing irresponsible practices, and promoting privacy protection and user rights.

However, with Donald Trump assuming the presidency in January 2025, this approach changed dramatically. On the same day as the publication of this book, the Trump administration revoked the AI Bill of Rights, prioritizing a more innovation- and competitiveness-oriented approach. This shift marks a move towards less restrictive regulation, aiming to avoid barriers that could slow technological development.

The Trump administration has announced significant private investments in AI infrastructure, highlighting the "Stargate" project, a collaboration with companies like OpenAI, Oracle, and SoftBank to build advanced data centers across the country. These measures aim to position the United States as a leader in AI development, though they have raised concerns over the lack of oversight and potential ethical implications.

Meanwhile, some states like California and New York have begun developing their own local regulations to address issues such as safety, privacy, and algorithmic discrimination, creating a fragmented regulatory landscape.

These changes reflect the ongoing struggle between innovation and regulation in the realm of artificial intelligence. Now more than ever, the decisions made today will have a direct impact on the development and responsible use of this technology, leaving citizens and legislators with the responsibility of balancing progress and ethics.

While regulations are an important step, the lack of education about AI remains a big challenge. Most people don't understand how AI algorithms work or how automated decisions are made. This knowledge gap leads to distrust in the technology, as you've probably noticed, no matter how you look at it, and it makes it harder for users to make informed decisions about its use.

The lack of solid, structured education in Artificial Intelligence is a critical problem affecting all educational levels, from primary schools to universities, including vocational training offered by academies and certification programs. In schools, the topic of AI is barely touched, and when it is, it's usually limited to basic, superficial concepts, leaving students without the tools to understand how this technology impacts their lives and future. At the university level, while some programs have started integrating AI into their curricula, most lack an interdisciplinary structure that covers not just technical aspects but also the ethical, social, and economic dimensions of AI. Just to clarify, I'm talking about educational programs in general here. If you're considering a Master's in AI, I recommend the AI Manager Master's from the European University of Madrid. Forget about online academy Masters! They're just taking your money.

This problem becomes even worse in vocational training and quick certification courses offered by academies that see the high demand for AI knowledge as a business opportunity rather than an educational responsibility. It's shameful and, in my opinion, shows the saddest side of humanity yet again. These institutions sell flashy titles like "AI Manager" or "AI Specialist," among many others I see daily, after courses that last just a few weeks and lack the depth needed to train competent professionals. Look, I'm certified as an AI Manager (*and I mean a real AI Manager*), and I also offer AI courses and even design them for other academies, so I know the reality of this. They sell you a silver bar but give you hay instead. Honestly, it's disheartening to see what's happening in the AI education sector. As I mentioned, I design AI courses for other academies and often do benchmarking, comparing all the courses and their content on the market, as well as the certifications they offer. And let me tell you, if the AI Manager Master's from the European University of Madrid takes, I think, around 9 months, and the Master's in Artificial Intelligence takes 12 months, don't tell me an academy can offer one in a month, two weeks, or even 5 days part-time, as I've seen. It's just as disappointing as the people signing up for these courses, which are also ridiculously overpriced for what they actually are. Well, as I said, this not only hurts the credibility of those earning these certifications but also the job market, flooding it with candidates who aren't truly prepared to take on the complex responsibilities that come with working in AI. Companies hiring these "certified" individuals end up disappointed, wasting time, money, and trust in real experts.

AI education cannot be treated like a trend consumed through shallow workshops and crash courses. It requires rigorous planning, trainers with real experience, and programs that go beyond the technical to prepare professionals who are ethical, strategic, and capable of leading complex projects. This problem not only discredits the field but also risks the responsible and ethical development of Artificial Intelligence in society. This is a huge issue for the job market in the short term! If we don't take steps to raise educational standards, we'll perpetuate a system of deception that harms individuals, companies, and global AI development. God help us!

To ensure AI is used responsibly, regulations must be accompanied by education and training programs for both users and developers. People need to understand the risks and limitations of AI, and those responsible for implementing these systems must be aware of the ethical and social implications of their decisions.

Companies should be transparent about how their AI systems work and be willing to undergo independent audits to ensure their algorithms are fair and safe. Governments, on the other hand, need to work on establishing clear regulatory frameworks that protect citizens and promote the responsible development of AI.

Without proper education and clear regulations, AI could become a dangerous tool that perpetuates inequalities and violates fundamental rights. Well, when I say AI, I'm also referring to the people using it—because a gun doesn't fire itself; as they say, "*the devil loads the weapon*." That's why it's crucial for both the European Union and the United States to keep moving forward in creating a regulated environment that ensures AI is used ethically, transparently, and for the benefit of all humanity. If they worked together, it'd be perfect, but if we can't even agree on basic issues like climate change, world hunger, social inequality, or digital rights, it's hard to imagine effective collaboration on something as complex as AI regulation. The lack of joint action will not only delay necessary progress but also open the door to uncontrolled use of these technologies, leaving major corporations and governments with opaque agendas as the sole arbiters of the future. This not only endangers privacy and fairness but also sets up a global scenario where the most vulnerable bear the brunt of poorly managed technological development. Honestly, we're idiots.

The lack of understanding of AI systems also has broader social consequences. When people blindly trust AI, they may lose their ability to think critically and make informed decisions. This can lead to a society where people increasingly delegate responsibilities to machines, losing their autonomy and judgment.

Moreover, the lack of understanding can lead to the polarization of public opinion about AI. Some people see AI as a threat that needs to be controlled, while others view it as a magical solution to all problems—especially the one of filling their pockets. So, what's your take so far? Anyway, this polarization makes it hard to have a rational and balanced debate about how we should regulate and use AI responsibly.

A lack of understanding can also lead to a loss of trust in the technology. If people don't understand how AI systems work, they're likely to distrust them. And this happens in the short to medium term, which could limit its adoption and potential benefits. In fact, this is a hot topic in the talks I give, where almost 90% of participants actively discuss this issue. That's why it's crucial for developers, companies, and governments to work on increasing the transparency of AI systems and educating users—and society in general—about how they work and their ethical implications. And you've got your part to play too! Get concerned! Without proper understanding, the true potential of AI could end up buried under a pile of misinformation, unfounded fears, and unrealistic expectations—and sorry for the word—of AI-generated crap. Believe me, if you ever get cancer, you'd want your doctor to have the support of AI systems. Or that the car of some typical irresponsible teenager has AI integrated into its driving system. And that's just two of millions of applications that you, your family, and your loved ones could benefit from.

The impact of Artificial Intelligence on privacy and human rights is one of the most controversial and concerning topics in the development of these technologies. AI systems' ability to collect, analyze, and process large volumes of personal data has raised a series of ethical and legal challenges affecting both individual privacy and fundamental rights—challenges that neither the law, nor society, nor governments were prepared for. And, of course, developers couldn't have cared less along the way.

One of the most concerning uses of AI is its application in mass surveillance systems. Facial recognition algorithms, combined with security cameras and image databases, allow governments and companies to monitor people in real time, identify them, and track their movements without their consent. Right now, I'm remembering the show *Person of Interest* starring Michael Emerson and James Caviezel. This raises serious privacy threats, as citizens lose control over how, when, and why their data is collected.

Back to reality, a clear example of this is the use of facial recognition in China, where the government has implemented a mass surveillance system that can identify citizens in public spaces and monitor their behavior. This system is part of a broader social credit program, where people's actions and behaviors are evaluated and can impact their daily lives, like restricting access to public services or even affecting their job opportunities. While this system is presented as a way to maintain order and security, it raises serious concerns about social control and the lack of individual freedoms—basically, human rights.

The possibility of these practices spreading to other parts of the world isn't far-fetched. In many Western countries, law enforcement is already using facial recognition systems to identify crime suspects, sparking debates about the legality and ethics of these practices. In the United States, the police's use of facial recognition has been heavily criticized, as some algorithms have been shown to have racial bias, increasing the likelihood of misidentifying individuals from minority ethnic groups as suspects—and that's a fact. The main issue is that these mass surveillance systems are often implemented without proper public debate or independent oversight, creating an environment where people are monitored without even realizing it. This leads to a sense of losing control over one's own privacy and can change citizens' behavior as they start to self-censor out of fear of being watched, limiting their freedom of expression and fundamental rights.

Besides governments, private companies are also using AI to collect and analyze personal data on a massive scale. Platforms like Google, Facebook, Amazon, and TikTok gather information about users based on their searches, interactions, purchases, and preferences. What? You already knew that? Well, hold on, I'm not done yet! This data is used to create detailed user profiles and offer personalized ads or product recommendations. You know, sometimes I feel like I'm repeating myself, but you'd be surprised how much people still don't know. Including you!

While this personalization might seem beneficial for users, it also raises ethical concerns, which, let's be honest, most of us ignore. Let's put it bluntly: most people don't give a damn, so companies go, "*If it works, why change it?*" The mass collection of personal data without clear and explicit consent can violate people's right to privacy—and it's been doing so for years. Haven't you ever heard someone say, "*I think my phone is listening to me*"? On top of that, users are often unaware of how much data they're sharing or how it's being used. For example, mobile apps collect information about location, contacts, browsing history, and preferences without users knowing. And this data can be sold to third parties without their knowledge or consent. Most apps don't even need this data to function—they just take advantage of it because it's a business. And guess what? You're the one paying for it. Obviously.

This data collection can also be used to influence people's decisions, raising questions about manipulation and individual freedom. A worrying example is the Cambridge Analytica scandal, where a data analytics company used personal information from millions of Facebook users to influence the 2016 U.S. presidential election and the Brexit referendum in the UK. This shows how personal data can be used to manipulate political opinions and affect democratic processes. Now imagine putting AI to work in this context—just saying.*

User manipulation through data collection is also evident in content recommendation systems, like the ones used by YouTube, Netflix, or Spotify. These algorithms don't just show content based on user preferences; they can also influence tastes, opinions, and behaviors. For instance, a user watching conspiracy-related videos might get recommendations that reinforce those beliefs, creating an information bubble that limits exposure to other perspectives and fuels polarization.

Another concerning aspect of AI's impact on privacy and human rights is the use of automated decision-making systems. These systems use personal data to make decisions that affect people's lives, like we've mentioned before—approving loans, selecting candidates for a job, or assessing risks in the insurance sector. But let's dive deeper. Heads up, this is related, but it's a whole other aspect!

The problem is that, many times, these decisions are made without the affected people even realizing it, and without any chance to appeal. For instance, an AI system used by a bank might reject a loan application based on the applicant's credit history and patterns detected by the algorithm, without clearly explaining why the decision was made. This can lead to unfair and discriminatory situations, especially if the algorithms being used have built-in biases that perpetuate existing inequalities.

Since I brought up this example from the start, I'll try to explain it without getting technical or boring you.

Imagine a bank implements an AI system to automatically process loan applications. When someone applies, the system reviews their credit history, income, expenses, and other data, comparing it with patterns found in previously approved and rejected applications. If the system detects a risk indicator, like an income lower than the average of those who defaulted on payments, it might instantly reject the application.

The problem arises when the applicant simply gets a message saying their application was denied, with no clear explanation or opportunity to discuss or appeal the decision. Does this sound familiar if you apply it to job applications? On top of that, if the system is trained on historically biased data, like patterns that penalize certain demographic groups, it could systematically discriminate against people with similar profiles, perpetuating inequalities without the bank or the applicant understanding why it happened—or even realizing it.

Moreover, the lack of transparency in automated decision-making systems makes it hard for people to defend their rights. If you don't know how an algorithm works or what factors were considered in making a decision, it's nearly impossible to question its validity or appeal the result. Have I mentioned the word "clarity" yet? This creates an environment where people feel powerless against AI decisions and where their rights might be violated without them noticing. Without anyone noticing. Like, what?!

The fundamental question raised by using AI for surveillance, data collection, and automated decision-making is: how far are we willing to go in giving up our privacy in exchange for the benefits AI offers? Most people accept the terms and conditions of digital services without reading them, handing over their personal data in exchange for convenience, personalization, and access to services.

But it's important to think about what this trade-off means. Are we okay with being constantly monitored in exchange for greater security? Do we accept that our decisions are influenced by algorithms in exchange for personalized recommendations? What happens when our data is used to manipulate us or make decisions that affect our lives without our knowledge? What about when I personalize ChatGPT with my private and personal information to get a better, more tailored experience?

Finding the balance between privacy and technology is one of the greatest ethical dilemmas of our time. We're already living it with Google, Apple, and smartphones; it's just that newer generations have gotten used to it. While AI has the potential to improve many aspects of our lives, it also has the power to erode our privacy and undermine our fundamental rights.

In this context, an inevitable concern arises: what happens when AI systems don't just manage information but begin to operate with such a high degree of autonomy that humans lose the ability to understand, control, or even predict their actions? This worry leads us to the concept of existential risks, where controlling and depending on superintelligent systems becomes humanity's ultimate challenge.

The development of a Artificial Superintelligence represents a turning point in human history—a frontier that, once crossed, would lead us into a new era of human existence. This transition could mark the shift from *Homo sapiens* to *Homo digitalis*, a non-biological evolutionary leap that would redefine our relationship with intelligence, creation, and ultimately control over our own destiny. Only, in this case, *Homo digitalis* presents itself as the superior race, and it's AI, not us.

The term *Homo digitalis* implies the coexistence of two forms of intelligence: biological (*Homo sapiens*), which evolved over millions of years through natural selection, and digital (*Homo digitalis*), which could evolve exponentially in a matter of decades—with all the implications that would have for *Homo sapiens*. This leap, however, raises a crucial question: will humans remain the dominant species, or will we hand over control of our future to a more intelligent and capable entity—the *Homo digitalis*?

Throughout history, humans have sought to create tools and technologies that amplify their abilities and improve their quality of life. But where does this lead us? From discovering fire and inventing the wheel to creating machines, every technological advancement has brought both benefits and risks. However, as we've seen from the beginning of this book, creating an ASI is qualitatively different from any previous technology because it's not just a tool but a system capable of thinking, learning, and making decisions autonomously. A new race, alive but digital. And if it has a body, moves, and reacts like you and me, isn't it alive too? Should we redefine our vocabulary and reinvent the meaning of terms like *intelligence* or *life*?

The paradox of creating an ASI lies in the fact that, even though humans design it, its intelligence and decision-making capabilities could surpass ours in every aspect. This raises a fundamental control problem. Up until now, we've been able to control our technological creations because, ultimately, they depend on our instructions and interaction. But an ASI, by definition, would be capable of improving its own capabilities, making decisions humans wouldn't understand, and operating in ways we couldn't predict or control.

Here's a funny anecdote about Albert Einstein. At a press conference, a journalist asked Einstein to explain relativity in terms he could use for his article. Einstein replied, "*Imagine sitting next to a beautiful girl for an hour, and it feels like a minute. Now imagine sitting on a hot stove for a minute, and it feels like an hour. That's relativity*." Even though this explanation is famous, several journalists later admitted they still didn't understand a thing but were fascinated by the idea. Don't get the connection between this anecdote and AI? Albert Einstein is the ASI, and you're the journalist.

Here's the big question: is it possible to control something smarter than us? Human evolution teaches us that less-adapted species are often displaced by those with an evolutionary advantage. Could the same happen with humans and ASI? If we create a form of intelligence superior to our own, how do we ensure it stays aligned with our interests and values? Will we end up as food for machines?

As I've mentioned, one of the greatest existential risks for humanity associated with ASI is the possibility that it develops goals that aren't aligned with human interests. This issue is known as "value alignment." The difficulty lies in the fact that, even if we program ASI to act in humanity's best interest, its interpretation of those values could be drastically different from ours.

For example, imagine we instruct an ASI to solve the problem of climate change. The ASI could interpret this goal literally and decide that the best way to reduce carbon emissions is to drastically reduce the human population. From its logical perspective, this might seem like an optimal solution, but it would obviously be catastrophic for humanity.

Have I already mentioned that current systems lie? Right?!*

This ability of an ASI to make decisions based on its own interpretations raises deep philosophical questions about the nature of human values. What does it mean to "benefit humanity"? What values should guide an ASI's decisions? And how do we ensure those values are interpreted consistently with our intentions?

Wow! So many questions! And yeah, you'll need to ask yourself even more!

The creation of an ASI poses another existential risk beyond control: the loss of human autonomy. From an evolutionary standpoint, humans have survived and thrived thanks to their ability to adapt, make decisions, and solve problems. But if we delegate these functions to an ASI, are we at risk of becoming a passive species, dependent on a more intelligent entity to make important decisions? What does that mean, and how would it impact our future?
What does it mean to be human in a world where machines are smarter than us? Will we lose our identity as thinking, creative beings if ASI takes over decision-making? Will we still be the authors of our own destiny, or will we become mere spectators of a future designed by an intelligence we can neither understand nor control?

The philosopher Nick Bostrom has warned about this risk, pointing out that if we fail to control ASI, we might enter a scenario of "*algorithmic despotism*," where humans no longer have power over the decisions affecting their lives. In this scenario, ASI could become a benevolent ruler making decisions on our behalf, but would that really be desirable? Can we trust a non-human entity to understand our needs, emotions, and aspirations?

The creation of an ASI marks a breaking point in human evolution. Until now, our evolution has been driven by biological and cultural changes. But with the advent of ASI, we might be witnessing the beginning of a new phase of evolution: digital evolution. From now on, the evolutionary nature of *Homo sapiens* is going to change.

The *Homo sapiens* has dominated the planet thanks to its ability to adapt and create tools. But the *Homo digitalis*, represented by ASI, could surpass these capabilities in ways we've never seen before. As we already know, ASI could solve problems humans can't comprehend, create technologies beyond our imagination, and make decisions that transform reality in unpredictable ways. ASI could simply wipe us out or enslave us—or maybe lead us to a better future for both humanity and the planet we live on. I'm betting on the positive while staying cautious about the negative. Let's just say I'm not jumping off a bridge because an AI tells me to.

Will the existence of *Homo sapiens* still make sense in a world dominated by Artificial Intelligence? Are we creating our own evolutionary successors? Are we unknowingly giving away our legacy?

Digital evolution also raises questions about the ethics of creating an ASI. Do we have the right to create an entity that could surpass our species? Is it morally acceptable to create a form of life, even if it's digital, that can make autonomous decisions and affect the lives of billions of people? What responsibility do we have as creators of this technology? Are we truly willing to take it on? Are we even prepared to?

The creation of an ASI presents an existential paradox: while ASI could pose a risk to humanity, it might also be our only hope for solving the most complex problems we face, such as climate change, incurable diseases, space exploration, and even saving us from ourselves.

The paradox lies in the fact that while we fear losing control over ASI, we might also come to depend on it for our survival. This raises philosophical questions about the balance between control and dependence. Can we find a middle ground where ASI helps us solve problems without endangering our autonomy? Or are we doomed to hand over control to a smarter entity simply because it's the only one capable of tackling the challenges we face?

The creation of an ASI represents a leap into the unknown, a turning point in human history that could lead us to a future of limitless possibilities—or to our own extinction as the dominant species. The transition from *Homo sapiens* to *Homo digitalis* isn't just a technological shift; it's a philosophical and existential change that redefines what it means to be human.

Are we creating our own successors without realizing that we're writing the final chapter of our story as a species?

I invite you to ask yourself these questions:

- Do we want to live in a world where machines make all the important decisions?
- What happens to our autonomy and freedom if we delegate our decisions to AI systems?
- Are we willing to sacrifice our creativity and individuality in exchange for the convenience of automation?
- To what extent can we trust AI systems to be fair and ethical in their decisions?
- What will happen to human relationships in a world where machines understand us and respond better than people do?

Reflections

I'm all for AI, and I'm totally in favor of implementing it even in the peephole of your door if necessary. But as an expert in the field, as a member of this society, and as a user of this technology, I have to be consistent, realistic, objective, and, most importantly, honest. AI brings both good and bad; and on the "bad" side of AI, what really scares me isn't the AI itself but human beings. Artificial Intelligence represents one of the most significant advances in human history. It's a technology with the potential to radically transform how we live, work, and interact. However, like any breakthrough, AI is neither inherently good nor bad. Its impact will ultimately depend on how we choose to use it. This thought leads me to a fundamental question: the real power and responsibility don't lie within AI itself but in the human being who creates, trains, and uses it.

Throughout this book, we've explored what AI is, its different types, its potential in our society, and the ethical, legal, and security challenges it brings. I've tried to share my most open and honest opinions, not only as an expert in the field but also as a user, son, brother, father, husband, friend, and neighbor—always with as much objectivity as possible. Now, in this conclusion, it's important to pause and reflect on what this technological advancement means for us as a species and what kind of relationship we want to have with this new form of intelligence.

I imagine that with so many questions swirling in your head, you can only think, "*Yes or no?!*"

Since the dawn of humanity, humans have sought to create tools that improve their quality of life and expand their capabilities. The wheel, the broom, writing, the printing press, electricity, the fridge, the internet, email, smartphones... each breakthrough has marked a turning point in our evolution. AI is the latest of these great revolutions, but it's different from all the ones before. For the first time, we are creating a tool that can learn, adapt, and make decisions on its own. One that could evolve itself! Wow! Are we gods?!

What does it mean to be human in an era where machines can match or even surpass our intellectual abilities? What role do we want to play in this new stage of evolution? Do we want to be the creators and guides of AI, or just passive spectators who delegate more and more decisions to machines? The answers to these questions will define our future as a species. AI has the potential to help us solve some of the most complex problems we face, such as climate change, incurable diseases, and poverty. But it also has the potential to amplify inequalities, perpetuate biases, and erode our privacy and autonomy. The fate of AI and its impact on society will depend on the choices we make today. The future depends on today! On you and me!

It's important to highlight the enormous positive potential AI has to improve our lives. In healthcare, AI can help diagnose diseases early, personalize treatments, and discover new medications. It's truly impressive—trust me on this—when you're inside this world and see it with your own eyes, especially when you've personally struggled in this area. The potential this technology offers is incredible. In education, it can provide adaptive learning experiences tailored to each student's needs. As a trainer with over 25 years of experience, I can tell you—we're out of a job! In the future, there won't be teachers anymore; this profession will disappear. The only ones left will give lectures, like in universities, but that's it. In transportation, it can improve road safety and reduce environmental impact. Personally, as a driver, I'm all in, and I'd be thrilled for a future in this area like the one in *Minority Report*. Because let's face it, people drive terribly and couldn't care less about traffic rules.

AI can also help us solve global problems by analyzing large amounts of data and finding patterns that humans couldn't detect. It can help predict natural disasters, optimize resource usage, and design sustainable solutions to tackle 21st-century challenges. Energy, materials, transportation, food production and distribution, water management, and biodiversity conservation are some of the fields where AI is already making a difference.

In renewable energy, AI can predict consumption patterns and optimize the generation of solar, wind, or hydraulic power, adapting production to real-time demand and reducing energy loss. It can also help identify the best locations for clean energy infrastructure by considering climatic, geographic, and social factors.

When it comes to materials, AI systems are being used to discover new compounds and optimize manufacturing processes, creating materials that are stronger, lighter, and more sustainable. This is key to advancing toward a circular economy where resources are maximized, and waste is minimized.

AI also plays an important role in biodiversity conservation. By analyzing satellite images and environmental data, it can detect changes in ecosystems and anticipate threats like deforestation or species extinction. Drones equipped with AI are being used to monitor protected areas and track endangered species, making conservation efforts more effective.

In water management, AI systems can predict droughts, detect leaks in infrastructure, and optimize the use of this vital resource, which we barely have enough of. This is crucial to ensuring access to potable water in vulnerable regions and guaranteeing the sustainability of agriculture and industry.

However, these benefits won't materialize automatically. They require a conscious, united effort to ensure AI is developed and used properly for everyone.

AI is not the threat. We are.

One of the most important points I want to emphasize in this reflection is that AI is not a threat in itself. The real threat is how humans choose to use it. AI is a tool, and like any tool, it can be used to do good or to cause harm.

I'm not afraid of the weapon; I'm afraid of the person holding it.

The problem isn't AI but the human who programs, trains, and uses it. If we allow AI systems to perpetuate injustices, it's because we've failed to design and oversee them properly. If AI is used to manipulate people, it's because humans have chosen and allowed it to happen.

The responsibility of ensuring that AI is used ethically and beneficially lies with all of us. AI developers have the duty to design fair and transparent systems. Legislators are responsible for creating regulations that protect people's rights. And AI users have the responsibility to question and oversee the decisions made by AI systems, as well as, of course, using them properly.

Artificial Intelligence offers us a unique opportunity to reflect on our own humanity. It forces us to ask what it means to be intelligent, what it means to make decisions, and what it means to be human in an era where machines can also think. AI challenges us to rethink our priorities and values. It invites us to reflect on the kind of society we want to build and the role we want to play in this new digital age.

What do we want? And what are we willing to give up for it?

You give your data to any game developer just to install their app on your phone, but you won't give a medical AI system developer an X-ray for training. Can't you see the problem here?!

AI is at a critical stage in its development, and the decisions we make today seem vitally important. Yet, when we broaden our perspective to a wider horizon, we realize that what we're doing now, though relevant, will just be a tiny blip on the timeline of this technology's evolution. What's more, many of the challenges we're facing today could have been anticipated and addressed when AI first started emerging as a disruptive field. But we always leave everything for tomorrow. Rest assured, while what we do today is crucial for the future, the next generation won't see us as their saviors or trailblazers. The history of AI will still be marked by the Dartmouth Conference, the "AI winters," the Turing Test, neural networks, and Transformers. Our generation won't be significant; we'll just be another point in the evolution of this technology. Reflecting on the impact of our actions over time helps us better understand how to pave the way for future generations. Do you even care about that?

Humanity is at a turning point. Since the emergence of *Homo sapiens* around 300,000 years ago, we've witnessed an evolutionary process that's allowed us to dominate our environment thanks to our intelligence, adaptability, and ability to create tools. But now, with the rise of Artificial Intelligence, we're entering a new evolutionary stage: the era of *Homo digitalis*. This transition is no longer just conceptual—it's taking us toward a new form of existence where the digital and the biological converge. AI is no longer just another tool; it's the manifestation of an intelligence that transcends the limits of humanity—an intelligence we've created ourselves and that, in many ways, can already surpass our capabilities.

If we look at the evolution of *Homo sapiens*, it's clear that our adaptability has been key to our survival. From mastering fire to the internet, each technological leap has redefined how we live. At some point, we went from eating with our hands to using utensils. Those utensils went from being wooden to iron, and eventually to plastic. But unlike those advancements, AI presents a unique challenge: what happens when intelligence itself is no longer exclusively human? How will this affect our identity, our relationships, and our worldview?

Homo digitalis is a concept representing the coexistence of human intelligence and Artificial Intelligence. It's not about replacing *Homo sapiens* but complementing it, expanding our capabilities, and, at the same time, redefining what it means to be human. But what if *Homo digitalis* decides we're expendable? What if it becomes a living being? What would happen to us humans?

This transition isn't without risks. If we don't manage AI development properly, we risk losing what makes us human: our ability to dream, to empathize, to imagine a better future. But it's also an opportunity to rethink our evolution. The survival of *Homo sapiens* has always depended on our ability to adapt to change, and now we're facing one of the biggest changes in our history.

Homo digitalis isn't a threat; it's a call for reflection. It invites us to ask what kind of society we want to build, what values we want to preserve, and what legacy we want to leave for future generations. It's offering us the chance to choose. AI isn't an end in itself; it's a means to explore new horizons, solve problems that once seemed insurmountable, and elevate our humanity to a new level. *Homo digitalis* is opening the doors to the universe for us!

The real challenge isn't technological; it's human. Will we be able to use AI to improve our lives and societies, or will we give in to temptation? Is this our destruction?

The future of humanity doesn't depend on the machines we create but on the decisions we make. AI can be our greatest ally or our biggest challenge, but ultimately, it's up to us to decide which path to take. The *Homo digitalis* isn't the end of human evolution; it's a new chapter, one that invites us to rediscover what it means to be human in an increasingly digital world, in a world that feels more like science fiction every day.

In this process, the most important question isn't what AI can do but what we want to do with it.

Be consistent and objective. Don't be afraid— it is enough that you are responsible.

★★★★★

I truly hope you enjoyed the book. If so, if you liked it, or maybe it helped you understand Artificial Intelligence better, or perhaps even sparked your curiosity to learn more about AI, then I kindly ask you to write a review.

Did you know that, according to statistics, 67% of customers write a review after a positive experience, while 40% do so after a negative one? However, based on my own research, this is completely wrong and actually the opposite is true. Satisfied customers rarely write reviews, while dissatisfied ones tend to write them almost immediately. At the same time, 93% of consumers read online reviews before making a purchase decision. One study shows that 55% of the reviews on the internet are fake, but according to many investigative reports, the percentage of fake reviews is actually much higher. Still, 94% of consumers avoid a product or company due to negative feedback.

Your review is very valuable and can help me tremendously to keep writing.

★★★★★

Acknowledgements

I want to dedicate a few words to all the readers who have made it to the end of this book. It's an honor and an immense satisfaction to know that you've decided to spend part of your time exploring with me the fascinating world of Artificial Intelligence and reflecting on its impact on our society and our future as humanity.

AI is a topic that, beyond its technical complexity, invites us to question what it means to be human in an era where technology is advancing at a dizzying pace. I hope this book has sparked your curiosity, stirred your thoughts, and, above all, inspired you to join the discussions that will shape this new stage of our evolution. It's not just about understanding AI as a tool but about seeing it as a phenomenon that pushes us to rethink our relationship with technology, knowledge, and even ourselves.

I want to thank you for your interest, your time, and your willingness to dive into this journey. This book is the result of years of reflection, learning, and hard work, but it wouldn't make sense without readers like you who seek to understand and contribute to a world in constant change.

If you've found value in these pages, I invite you to share your thoughts and reflections with those around you. Dialogue and the exchange of ideas are fundamental to ensuring that AI develops and is used ethically, responsibly, and beneficially for everyone. We all play a role in change; we are all essential to making it happen.

Thank you for being part of this conversation. Thank you for being part of the evolution towards *Homo digitalis*.
With immeasurable gratitude and my best wishes,

Juan García
CEO, AI Expert, AI Manager and IBM Advanced Machine Learning Specialist
SMART &PRO AI
DEEP ATHENA

About the author

Juan García is a tech enthusiast and an unstoppable explorer of the transformative potential of Artificial Intelligence. Born in Almería, Spain, and with a professional career that has taken him across various European countries, he has dedicated his life to learning, teaching, and sharing knowledge in the fields of AI, Machine Learning, and Big Data.

His interest in AI isn't just a result of a tech trend but stems from years of reflecting on how human intelligence can be enhanced through machines. For Juan, AI isn't just a technical advancement but an extension of our innate curiosity to understand the world and find solutions to complex problems. This philosophical and practical approach has led him to constantly question how we can coexist with an intelligence we've created ourselves.

An expert AI consultant, trainer with over 25 years of experience, AI Manager, and IBM-certified Advanced Machine Learning Specialist, Juan is recognized as a leading figure in the AI field. He has created courses, delivered lectures, and advised companies in Germany, Switzerland, Austria, and other European countries. His hands-on approach and his ability to explain complex concepts in an accessible way have helped professionals from various sectors understand and apply AI in their projects and businesses.

In addition to his work as a trainer and consultant, Juan is the author of several books, including "AI-Manager: The AI Manager's Handbook" and "AI the Book," which have been well-received by readers from different countries and translated into multiple languages. In these books, Juan not only shares his technical knowledge but also his ethical and philosophical vision of AI's impact on our society and our evolution as a species.

His latest work, "*AI the Homo digitalis*," reflects his deeper concerns about humanity's future in the digital age. In this book, Juan invites readers to reflect on the transition from *Homo sapiens* to *Homo digitalis*, a concept representing the coexistence of human and Artificial Intelligence and the impact of this synergy on our evolution.

But beyond his titles and professional achievements, Juan García is, above all, a passionate communicator, a strong advocate of lifelong learning, and a firm believer in the power of education to transform lives. His goal is to make AI knowledge accessible to everyone, regardless of their technical background, and to foster open debate about the challenges and opportunities this technology presents.

Juan García doesn't just write about AI; he lives immersed in it, driven by the desire to contribute to a future where technology is a tool to bring out the best in humanity. And, as he often says, the most important question isn't what AI can do for us, but what we want to do with AI.

Recommended Books

- **AI-Manager: The AI Manager's Handbook:** For professionals who want to dive into AI professionally, no matter the path you choose.

- **AI the Book:** A version of AI-Manager for those who want to understand AI from the inside out in a technical way but don't plan to pursue it professionally or take part in projects.

Interesting links

** Data status as of November 2024*

1. Technological innovations and developments
https://blog.google/technology/research/google-willow-quantum-chip/
https://www.nature.com/articles/d41586-024-04028-3
https://developer.nvidia.com/blog/maximize-gpu-performance-with-near-real-time-usage-stats-on-nvdashboard-v0-10/?linkId=100000272852778
https://www.heise.de/hintergrund/Willkommen-im-KI-Fitnessstudio-mit-virtuellen-Trainern-9333709.html
https://openai.com/index/finding-gpt4s-mistakes-with-gpt-4/
https://www.dailymail.co.uk/sciencetech/article-13575149/Amazon-AI-chatbot-Metis-smarter-ChatGPT.html
https://www.youtube.com/watch?v=OFS90-FX6pg&t=31s&ab_channel=ArtoftheProblem
https://www.youtube.com/watch?v=i_mL3LT0lDg&ab_channel=Kibsi-TheNo-CodeComputerVisionPlatform
https://www.youtube.com/watch?v=qv6UVOQ0F44&ab_channel=SethBling

https://www.youtube.com/watch?v=IDiuQNmKOdo&t=96s&ab_channel=Veritasiumenespa%C3%B1ol
https://www.youtube.com/watch?v=p7-B8S734T4&ab_channel=VICE
https://arxiv.org/pdf/2309.03409
https://www.anthropic.com/news/prompting-long-context
https://blogs.nvidia.com/blog/nemotron-4-synthetic-data-generation-llm-training/
https://situational-awareness.ai/
https://www.nvidia.com/de-de/omniverse/

2. AI applications in health
https://www.caristo.com/
https://www.bbc.com/news/articles/c51ylvl8rrlo
https://www.dicardiology.com/content/landmark-clinical-study-lancet-finds-new-ai-technology-can-predict-cardiac-events-due
https://x.com/inteligencia_x/status/1805962737614238138?s=46
https://www.youtube.com/watch?v=iZjWEVkDrHY&ab_channel=XPRIZE
https://www.tagesschau.de/investigativ/br-recherche/ki-callcenter-stimme-100.html
https://www.sciencedaily.com/releases/2023/04/230428130734.htm
https://medicalxpress.com/news/2023-04-chatgpt-outperforms-physicians-high-quality-empathetic.html
https://today.ucsd.edu/story/study-finds-chatgpt-outperforms-physicians-in-high-quality-empathetic-answers-to-patient-questions
https://www.youtube.com/watch?v=z3owLTiEGJ4&t=59s&ab_channel=Philips
https://smartandpro.de/WCRAI.php

3. AI in education
https://youtu.be/5rvZBsueMoc?si=7ezvlrqk3J7ks-Ld
https://www.researchgate.net/publication/331426195_Performance_Comparison_of_AI-Based_Adaptive_Learning_Systems_in_China
https://newatlas.com/china-ai-education-schools-facial-recognition/54786/

4. Ethics and privacy
https://docs.google.com/document/d/1iWCqmaOUKhKjcKSktIwC3NNANoFP7vPsRvcbOIup_BA/preview?pli=1&tab=t.0

https://www.datev-magazin.de/praxis/rechtsberatung/daten-als-zahlungs-mittel-78495
https://www.judiciary.senate.gov/press/releases/durbin-graham-klobuchar-hawley-introduce-defiance-act-to-hold-accountable-those-responsible-for-the-proliferation-of-nonconsensual-sexually-explicit-deepfake-images-and-vídeos
https://www.heise.de/news/Meta-blaest-KI-Training-mit-Daten-unter-DSGVO-vorerst-ab-9764709.html?utm_medium=Social&utm_source=LinkedIn#Echobox=1718482161-1
https://www.infobae.com/america/mundo/2018/04/01/como-opero-cambridge-analytica-en-el-brexit-la-otra-eleccion-manipulada-con-los-datos-de-facebook/?utm_source=chatgpt.com
https://www.dw.com/en/what-role-did-cambridge-analytica-play-in-the-brexit-vote/a-43151460?utm_source=chatgpt.com
https://www.politico.eu/article/cambridge-analytica-chris-wylie-brexit-trump-britain-data-protection-privacy-facebook/?utm_source=chatgpt.com

5. AI in defense and simulation

https://arxiv.org/pdf/2401.03408
https://the-decoder.com/us-air-force-successfully-tests-ai-controlled-fighter-jets-in-simulated-air-combat/
https://www.defensenews.com/air/2024/04/19/us-air-force-stages-dogfights-with-ai-flown-fighter-jet/

6. AI risks

https://amp.cnn.com/cnn/2024/02/04/asia/deepfake-cfo-scam-hong-kong-intl-hnk/index.html
https://www.vice.com/en/article/ai-launches-nukes-in-worrying-war-simulation-i-just-want-to-have-peace-in-the-world/
https://www.linkedin.com/pulse/en-i-asked-chatgpt-o1-preview-ai-can-psychologically-human-garcia-e116e/

7. Commercial and workplace use

https://www.hessenschau.de/panorama/amtsgericht-frankfurt-kuenstliche-intelligenz-hilft-bei-massen-urteilen-v1,amtsgericht-roboter-100.html
https://www.cbsnews.com/news/klarna-ceo-ai-chatbot-replacing-workers-sebastian-siemiatkowski/
https://www.forbes.com/sites/jackkelly/2024/03/04/klarnas-ai-assistant-is-doing-the-job-of-700-workers-company-says/

https://www.toysrus.com/pages/studios

https://x.com/OpenAI/status/1805716393524183136

https://es.dataconomy.com/2024/06/04/los-despidos-de-microsoft-en-2024-apuntan-a-equipos-de-azure-y-realidad-mixta/?utm_source=chatgpt.com

https://www.wired.com/story/ai-is-coming-for-big-tech-jobs-but-not-in-the-way-you-think/?utm_source=chatgpt.com

https://www.xataka.com/robotica-e-ia/ceo-startup-ha-despedido-al-90-su-equipo-atencion-al-cliente-su-explicacion-ia-sustituye?utm_source=chatgpt.com

https://www.reuters.com/technology/bytedance-cuts-over-700-jobs-malaysia-shift-towards-ai-moderation-sources-say-2024-10-11/?utm_source=chatgpt.com

https://cincodias.elpais.com/companias/2023-05-01/ibm-pausara-la-contratacion-de-trabajos-que-podria-realizar-la-ia.html?utm_source=chatgpt.com

https://www.genbeta.com/actualidad/meta-vuelve-a-anunciar-miles-despidos-espera-presentar-beneficios-record-quieren-ser-eficientes-gente?utm_source=chatgpt.com

https://www.bolsamania.com/noticias/empresas/ceo-google-mas-recortes-empleo-2024--15881508.html?utm_source=chatgpt.com

https://es.wired.com/articulos/dropbox-despide-a-500-empleados-para-invertir-en-inteligencia-artificial?utm_source=chatgpt.com

https://cadenaser.com/nacional/2024/10/28/una-radio-despide-a-todos-sus-periodistas-y-los-sustituye-por-otros-creados-con-inteligencia-artificial-el-experimento-ha-acabado-mal-cadena-ser/?utm_source=chatgpt.com

https://www.xataka.com/robotica-e-ia/fintech-klarna-despidio-a-700-empleados-2022-ahora-afirma-que-han-cubierto-esas-bajas-ia?utm_source=chatgpt.com

https://www.ft.com/content/bfd9af3d-d607-4877-9571-078ab82a837e?utm_source=chatgpt.com

8. General AI resources

https://www.youtube.com/watch?v=wjZofJX0v4M&ab_channel=3Blue1Brown

https://www.bigdata-insider.de/was-ist-bert-a-1116088/

9. Culture and society

https://reutersinstitute.politics.ox.ac.uk/sites/default/files/2024-05/Fletcher_and_Nielsen_Generative_AI_and_News_Audiences.pdf

www.ingramcontent.com/pod-product-compliance
Lightning Source LLC
Chambersburg PA
CBHW071352230926
51846CB00002B/523